UNLOCK YOUR CALL CENTRE

A proven way to upgrade security, efficiency and caller experience

MATT SMALLMAN

Rethink

First published in Great Britain in 2022 by Rethink Press
(www.rethinkpress.com)

To my best friend, soulmate and wife, Charlie, without whose unwavering support I'd never have started, let alone finished.

Contents

Foreword

Julius Caesar is credited with coining the adage, 'Experience is the teacher of everything' (*Ut est rerum omnium magister usus*). Today, I would argue that learning from the experience of others is often the better approach, because it enables a person to avoid common mistakes and pitfalls that were exposed by one's predecessors.

As the founder of Opus Research, a technology analysis firm specialising in conversational commerce, I've tracked the evolution of technologies that support trusted conversations between companies and their customers. In 2003, we were commissioned by a major telecom carrier to conduct a worldwide study of the potential to use voice biometrics to simplify and accelerate the processes required to authenticate citizens calling into its country's tax authority. Thus started my decade's interest in the combination of methods that governments, financial institutions, telecom carriers, healthcare providers and retailers might use to support continuous, seamless and friction-free customer authentication.

While I was an interested third party to the development of what I call Intelligent Authentication (IAuth), Matt was at the coalface of implementing voice biometrics at major UK-based financial institutions. We first met at Opus Research's Voice Biometrics Conference in Amsterdam in 2011 when he was looking for the kind of best practice advice that this book provides – but which hasn't existed until now. We've stayed in touch ever since, and he has continued to provide a 'reality check' for many of our events and publications.

More recently, it has been my pleasure to work with Matt as we combine our different perspectives into the annual *Intelligent Authentication and Fraud Prevention Intelliview* issued jointly by Opus Research and SymNex Consulting, which describes the state of the market each year.

In this book, Matt provides insights, frameworks and prescriptions based on decades of experience, initially in the military and then as an executive and consultant to large financial institutions. Over the years he has designed and implemented solutions to the challenges that arise when those companies want to secure their call centres and protect their customers' financial assets from attacks originated by increasingly sophisticated and organised groups of imposters.

The title of the book, *Unlock Your Call Centre*, ironically encapsulates the challenges that call centres and security professionals collectively confront. Their companies must be totally open to engage in phone-based conversations with legitimate customers. At the same time, they must erect formidable barriers against concerted efforts by organised fraudsters, who are constantly upping their efforts to overcome time-tested authentication methods, especially the most vulnerable: the knowledge-based options, including PINs, passwords and challenge questions.

Matt starts with a deep dive into the challenges associated with current security methods, before introducing the modern security options for today's call centres. Throughout he makes an important distinction that has been a long time coming, because IAuth is much more than consumer identification and access management (CIAM). Authentication and fraud prevention in the call centre calls for sensitivity to customer experience (CX) and the emotional state of each caller.

Readers of this book will come away armed with an understanding of a broad range of options available to secure today's call centres. Most importantly, Matt provides detailed, step-by-step instructions for design, implementation and ongoing testing of modern security solutions, recognising that today's solutions must embrace multiple channels and modalities.

Following his advice and recommendations, readers will learn that the best way to unlock their call centres is to implement strong, yet effortless, authentication strategies to make them more secure, trustworthy and pleasing to customers.

Dan Miller
Opus Research (www.opusresearch.net)

Introduction

As a leader responsible for your organisation's call-centre experience, you almost certainly share the frustration of your customers and colleagues with the way security has evolved. You likely know that your mother's maiden name and date of birth are readily available to anyone who goes looking. At the same time, you struggle with the mental gymnastics of working out the seventh letter of your password or remembering how much your last bill was. Yet your own colleagues are probably asking those or similar questions hundreds of times every hour.

Your call centre needs to change, perhaps not as quickly or in the same way as some may expect, but it does need to evolve. Customers' expectations are changing; the proliferation of self-service tools and other channels means that call centres are relaying fewer facts and being asked to solve more problems. Customers aren't just seeking functional resolutions to their problems; they are looking for an emotional connection so they can trust call-centre staff and be confident they are making the right decisions. As a result, the type of people you need to meet these needs are changing as well.

It's possible that your current processes are getting in the way of you finding the right people. The sort of person who is good at empathising with customers and solving complex problems is not going to be satisfied denying service to a distressed customer because they couldn't remember their dog's inside leg measurement. It's tough for your frontline colleagues to build trust with customers when every call starts with a subconscious attitude that the caller isn't who they claim to be, driven by your colleague's fear of getting it wrong and losing their job.

Whether you're working in the public or private sector, with ten thousand agents or ten, handling high-value transactions or just booking appointments, there must be a better way than the old one. This book is that way. It will help you to unlock the potential of your call centre by getting the process out of the way without compromising security, minimising the effort customers and agents have to expend to prove callers are who they claim to be, reducing your cost to serve while, more importantly, allowing agents to build the connection with customers to meet the full range of their needs.

My journey

I found my way to call-centre security via the military. I joined the British Army just before 9/11, so my career was characterised by unconventional conflicts. My niche was developing and teaching military commanders the tactics required to prevent terrorists and their explosive devices from achieving their objectives. By combining the lessons of history with the available technologies of the day and understanding the enemy's psychology, we were able to solve this seemingly impossible problem.

A decade later, I found myself responsible for improving the efficiency and experience of a bank's complex international call centre. In this role, I was constantly struck by how the company's security processes were getting in the way of my colleagues building a relationship with their customers, and they were still letting fraudsters through. Convinced there must be a better way, I tried everything possible to improve the existing processes before realising that an entirely different approach was required.

Taking inspiration from the best in-person experiences of five-star hotels and restaurants, combined with the traditions of local bank branches and stores,

I came to believe that the best security experience was one that customers don't even notice; one where they are recognised by name and feel trusted from the first moment without needing to do anything other than show up. In trying to figure out how we could achieve this in a remote call-centre context, I realised that it was not that the technologies didn't exist; it was that they hadn't been applied in a way consistent with this perspective, and they didn't demonstrate an understanding of customer and agent psychology.

As an employee, I made the case to senior executives, designed and implemented first-of-their-kind approaches to customer identification and authentication, won multiple awards for innovation and customer experience, and had a far more significant commercial impact than I ever expected. While the numbers spoke for themselves, it was the stories and genuine gratitude of frontline colleagues and customers that highlighted the importance of getting this seemingly simple process right. Later, frustrated by how few organisations had closed the gap between the possibilities of the technology and the reality of implementation, and how little had changed for customers in general, I started SymNex Consulting with a mission to make everyone's life just that little bit easier.

Along the way, I've learned more about human behaviour, fraudster tactics, machine learning, privacy law, audio processing, statistics and telephone signalling than any businessperson should. I'm not saying the road hasn't been bumpy (I've been laughed out of more than a few offices along the way), but I've navigated it enough times to show you where the pitfalls are and to realise that not everyone is starting from the same place, or even has the same destination in mind.

Your journey

The modern call centre is inundated with demands to do more: support a never-ending stream of business initiatives, be customer-focused, comply with the latest regulations and be a great place to work. Doing nothing about security may seem like the easy path, but it isn't. We waste so much time interrogating customers who are who they claim to be and asking questions that don't provide any real security. At the same time, bad actors are circumventing our controls to steal our customers' data and money without us even knowing. There is a clear cost to the status quo, hidden from many, that constrains our ability to deliver on our modern-day demands.

You may be surprised how emotive this issue can be when you draw attention to it in the right way. Executives may never have experienced the painful bits of the process, let alone thought through the consequences. Security professionals will always be biased towards elimination of risk and resistant to upsetting the balance, but when you can make the implications of the status quo clear and prove that 'better' means better on every level, these sceptics can become some of your greatest advocates and supporters.

You don't need to spend an excessive amount of time and money to achieve better outcomes. The efficacy of modern security methods is proven, and their costs continue to fall as their accessibility increases. In many cases, 'better' may be using what you already have in another way.

Because the security process is a prerequisite for almost every call you take, it has an outsized impact on every measure of call-centre performance. It's rare in business that solving problems doesn't present trade-offs, but improving your call centre's security processes will deliver a real win-win-win. Technology enables you to deliver solutions that are genuinely better for customers, better for colleagues and better for the organisation.

The key to unlocking

This book gives you a step-by-step approach to enhancing your security while improving your customer's journey. Informed by experience and with access to a proven toolkit, it will show you how to assess your current processes' usability, efficiency and security so that you can make a compelling case for improvement. It will show you how to understand your customer and risk environment so that you can select the appropriate methods and mix them for your unique context. Finally, it will provide a framework to implement and sustain those methods.

In Chapter 1, we will decouple identification (the claim of identity) from authentication (proving the claim), which many organisations conflate into an amorphous security process, even though this blocks pragmatic discussion of alternatives. We will bust the myth of perfect security by exploring the trade-off between that and the convenience of different authentication methods, discovering how to achieve high confidence without high effort.

In Chapters 2 (Usability), 3 (Efficiency) and 4 (Security), we will explore each dimension of security-process performance to discover the real value of getting the process right. In Chapter 5, we will look at the specific issues of the traditional security methods, as well as more recently introduced transitional methods that have attempted to address some of these issues. Even if you are familiar with these issues, it's worth checking the summary of the chapter to refresh your memory.

In Chapter 6, I will introduce you to modern call-centre security, the key to unlocking your centre. This philosophy and approach use advances in technology to balance the competing demands of usability, efficiency and security. This chapter is key to understanding modern security, so even if you are more interested in implementing specific technologies, please don't skip it.

Chapter 7 will help you establish how your processes currently perform. Using this information alongside your unique context, covered in Chapter 8, you can then determine the appropriate modern methods and their mix in Chapter 9 to unlock your call centre's full potential.

In Chapter 10, we will use this plan to make the case to your wider organisation to gain the support and resources you need to deliver better solutions. I will share my experiences of what works and what doesn't from having done this countless times.

Chapter 11 goes into the detail of implementing this plan and designing the business processes needed to support the modern methods of voice biometrics, covered in Chapter 12, and network authentication, Chapter 13, to maximise customer acceptance and business value. We will conclude with a roadmap in Chapter 14, the result of hard lessons learned, so that you can switch on these services in the quickest and safest way possible. Finally, Chapter 15 will explore how to sustain them for the long term.

In short, this book, combined with the tools and references found at www.symnexconsulting.com/unlock-book, will equip you with everything you need to unlock your call centre's full potential.

PART ONE

WHY SECURITY MATTERS

If, like me, you know in your gut that your security processes aren't serving anyone, then you need to be able to explain the challenge in ways that resonate with your key stakeholders. This section is about understanding how you ended up here, the consequences of your current situation and a framework for telling that story and articulating the impact of doing better.

1
Fundamentals

We've ended up where we are for sound reasons. Our predecessors did the best job they could with the tools available to them. In this chapter, we'll explore their journey and the fundamental trade-off we still face today.

Evolution of security in customer service

Before we look at the modern call centre, it's helpful to go back in time and explore how security has evolved through the ages of customer service. In the beginning, all commercial relationships were conducted face to face and were almost entirely transactional.

Therefore, there was no need to know who the other party was claiming to be, let alone confirm that. If their money or whatever they were exchanging was good, then the deal could be done.

As commerce evolved, some relationships became less transactional and more enduring. Concepts such as credit and accounts came into being, even if they were only recorded in paper ledgers, but the number of parties involved was still relatively small. As a result, it was easy for proprietors and their employees to recognise their customers by their face, voice and other distinguishing features when they met.

As businesses grew, the number of people involved in any one transaction increased and the ledgers became bigger, often requiring some form of index, like an account number, to help employees find the customer's records. At this scale, it became almost impossible for employees to recognise every customer, so signatures were added to the ledger and used to confirm someone was who they claimed to be.

As enterprises became bigger, the number of their customers increased and personal relationships reduced. They also became an attractive target for criminals seeking to exploit weaknesses in their processes for personal gain. Enterprises responded by issuing cards, chequebooks and other identifying items that were harder to copy or obtain illicitly.

As technology evolved with the arrival of the phone and later the internet, and enterprises became even larger and more physically distant from their customers, the need to provide services remotely increased. To avoid criminal exploitation, enterprises developed mechanisms of securing transactions using secret information known only to the two legitimate parties. These started with questions about the customer and their relationship with the enterprise, but as enterprises increasingly sought to automate processes and formerly secret information became more readily available, they adopted the passwords and personal identification numbers (PINs) that we know today. Now we are dependent on this secret information as the primary means of security.

Each step in this evolution was perfectly rational and made best use of the technologies available at the time, but it took enterprises further away from really knowing their customers. It also made those customers do more work, often for short-lived gains in confidence and productivity.

The security/convenience trade-off

The evolution of security in customer service has been shaped by an age-old conundrum. The most convenient thing for any customer to do is just talk to, turn up at or write in to an organisation without any form of identification or authentication, but this is insecure and opens organisations up to a significant risk of fraud and malicious activity. As organisations have been forced to make their processes more secure, we have seen a corresponding reduction in convenience for the customers. Signing something is harder than just being yourself. Finding your chequebook is harder still – and remembering your dog's inside leg measurement is for many just too hard!

This trade-off can be represented graphically:

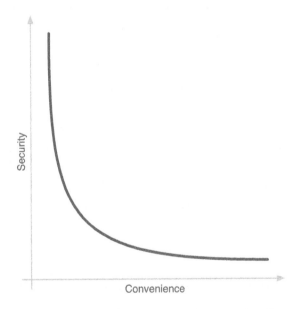

Figure 1.1: Security and convenience trade-off

As security increases, convenience decreases, and vice versa. What's more, as both security and convenience approach their highest levels, they have an outsized impact on each other. Beyond a certain point, getting a little bit more secure has a disproportionate impact on convenience. These lines never quite touch their axes, because if there were such a thing as a perfectly secure system, it would be perfectly inconvenient and unusable. Perfect security is therefore a myth.

While this curve is an oversimplification of reality, the general relationship does hold true. Every authentication method is capable of being plotted in this space. In practice, each method can be modified to make it slightly easier or harder to use, and more or less secure, to achieve something resembling the curve in Figure 1.2.

Figure 1.2: *Illustrative plot of security vs convenience of different authentication methods*

We all subconsciously trade off security for convenience in our daily lives. Here are a few examples.

Have you ever spent five minutes looking for your front door key in the bottom of your bag or every pocket? This is a classic security versus convenience trade-off. It's not convenient to have to stop and lock the door on your way out, carry a bunch of keys all day, and then be stuck outside in the cold trying to get into your warm home. But most of us do it because we value the security it provides. Of course, if you live somewhere remote, you may think nothing of leaving your door unlocked while you nip out because you don't perceive there to be a security risk and you want the convenience of not carrying keys.

Another example is standing in line at the airport, taking your shoes and belt off and emptying the contents of your washbag. I'm sure no one enjoys this, but would you get on an aircraft if you weren't sure everyone else had been through the same process? You are trading your convenience for security, or the perception of security, which we'll discuss later.

We probably all make similar trade-off decisions when coming home late at night. Do we take the convenient route along the dark alley or stick to the well-lit main road?

A two-tier process

It's important to understand what the security process needs to achieve to service customers. In most cases, the process addresses two conceptually different requirements:

Security = Identification + Authentication

Identification establishes which of the organisation's many customers this caller is claiming to be. It usually requires finding the unique record in the relevant systems that relates to the caller. This is the purpose of the account or customer number.

Authentication confirms (or verifies) that the caller is who they claim to be, to a sufficient level of confidence to allow an agent to carry out the caller's request. Today, this is usually achieved through confirming they know something only the genuine customer is supposed to know.

The real risk in call centres comes from authentication rather than identification. Anyone can claim to be someone else, but it's only when you incorrectly believe this assertion that it creates a risk for your organisation.

As remote service has evolved, these requirements have often been conflated in caller challenges that both identify and authenticate. A customer's date of birth, for example, is unlikely to be shared with many other customers, is likely to be remembered by the real customer and, up until recently, was unlikely to be known or widely available to others. As security processes evolved, using date of birth for both identification and authentication reduced the overall call time, so it seemed perfectly rational to do so. But it no longer provides the same level of authentication confidence that it did in the past, even though it remains a perfectly effective identification method.

In some call centres, there may be an additional security requirement known as identity verification (or proofing). This happens when a caller is not yet a customer of your organisation, so has no record. In this case, before providing goods or services, you need to confirm that the caller is both who they claim to be (authenticate) and a real person (prove), based on some external source, such as a government-issued identification document or a credit reference agency.

Authentication methods fall into one of three categories, known as factors. When authentication uses methods from more than one of these groups, it is known as multi-factor authentication.

- **Inherence** – authentication based on something you are. For example, a proprietor recognising a customer by their face, voice or signature. It depends on the uniqueness of the customer's physical or behavioural features and is often known as biometrics.

- **Possession** – authentication based on something you possess, such as a cheque book or identity card. It depends on an item issued to and controlled by the known customer.

- **Knowledge** – authentication based on something known only by the genuine customer and the organisation, such as the answers to personal questions, PINs and passwords.

All authentication factors and corresponding methods have their own strengths and weaknesses which we will explore in subsequent chapters. The 'right' factor is highly dependent on the context of use.

Dimensions of security-process performance

To assess the performance of your security process holistically, you need to consider it from more than one dimension. I assess performance against three dimensions:

- **Usability** – a broad term that includes convenience and experience, usability refers to how easy the process is for both consumers and employees to use. The security process is only a means to an end, and too much cognitive demand will frustrate both callers and agents and distract them from the real reason for the call. We will explore the different facets of usability in Chapter 2.

- **Efficiency** – this reflects the time taken up by the process, and therefore its cost and that of any subsequent fulfilment process it enables. For example, an automated identification and authentication process might be considered more efficient than one that requires agent intervention, especially if the former enables the caller to resolve their own query using a self-service application. We will explore efficiency further in Chapter 3.

- **Security** – this dimension reflects the confidence provided by the process that the caller is who they claim to be, thereby preventing fraudulent access to customer data and providing customers with reassurance that they are safe. In some cases, maintaining customer confidence can be more important than preventing fraudulent access. We will explore security further in Chapter 4.

The security process is most likely to feel broken to its participants and stakeholders when one or more of these dimensions is out of balance with the others. Consider these four examples that rely on customer input:

1. Callers are required to enter their social security number and online password (alphanumeric with complexity rules requiring special characters) into

an interactive voice response (IVR) system before speaking to an agent.

2. Callers are required to enter their customer identifier (sent during account opening, but rarely used in other communications) and subsequently an eight-digit one-time passcode (OTP) sent by short message service (SMS) to their registered mobile number into an IVR system before speaking to an agent.

3. Callers have a dedicated number which routes directly to a team of three to four agents who support their account (and often thousands of others). Callers identify themselves with their name and are recognised by the agents or are challenged for their mother's maiden name and date of birth.

4. Callers are asked their reason for calling, a specific part of their twelve-digit alphanumeric policy number, and then their date of birth as eight numbers by an IVR system before being connected with an agent. The agent subsequently asks them to confirm their mother's maiden name before discussing their claim.

Unfortunately, these examples are not fictitious. The first method is clearly attempting to be efficient, but requiring customers to enter a complex password using a touchtone keypad is highly prone to error, reducing its real efficiency while creating a significant cognitive load for the caller. This makes it hard to use and, because this same information is contained in another channel, it's not even that secure as it could easily be compromised there.

In the second case, the process is likely to be reasonably secure, relying on obscure information for identification and possession-based authentication, based on the assumption that only the genuine customer will get the text message. But this does make the process hard to use, especially if the customer is calling on the same device that the passcode is sent to. It's also unlikely to be that efficient if most callers need to speak to an agent because they have no idea what their customer identifier is.

In the third case, callers may well appreciate the ease of use of this process, but if they're asked to reflect on how they feel about the level of security, they are unlikely to be reassured. Because it is dependent on a small number of agents, it is probably not that efficient for the organisation, particularly during periods of heavy demand.

The final example provides little or no security, as all the information is likely to be easily obtainable, but it is hard for customers to complete, as most won't know their policy number and many remember their date of birth as six digits.

Summary

This chapter has given you an overview of the history and fundamentals of security in customer service. The key points we covered are:

- The security process is based on two elements: identification and authentication.

- There is a fundamental trade-off between convenience and security.

- The three different authentication factors are knowledge, possession and inherence.

- Three performance dimensions of the security process are usability, efficiency and security.

2
Usability

U sability is the primary performance dimension of the security process. Get it right and both security and efficiency flow, but usability is all wrapped up in human psychology. It's a complicated subject deeply linked to behaviour, not just that of customers, but also of call-centre agents.

Success and failure

While there are many aspects to the usability of a security process, the simplest measure is how often someone who is who they claim to be is able to complete it successfully. The inverse of this, and the source of greatest customer frustration, is known as a false reject (FR): a genuine caller who is unable to access the service because they can't successfully complete the security process.

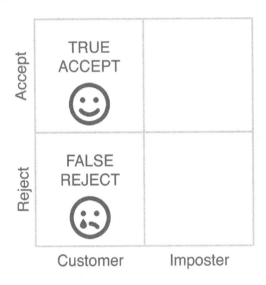

Figure 2.1: Customer security-process outcomes

Different identification and authentication methods will have different rates of FR depending on their design and the factors they use, but the overall usability of an organisation's process will also depend on how frequently each of these methods is used. If you work on the basis that nearly all callers to a call centre are who they claim to be, then the FR rate is simply the number of customers who are denied or restricted service as a result of failing to complete the process.

The most common reason for a caller failing to complete the security process is a difference between what they think the answer to a knowledge-based question is and what the organisation's system thinks it is. The caller may simply not be able to remember because the answer relates to something that happened a long time ago or is easily confused with similar information, or the information in the organisation's system may be wrong because it was mis-keyed, not updated when it should have been or somehow corrupted. In this case, it's easy for both sides to blame each other, but the result is usually that the customer must be denied or given only limited access to the service they are entitled to, even though they are who they claim to be.

Cognitive dissonance

Identity is a profoundly personal attribute and one that we think about a lot of the time. Questions about who we are, what we stand for and how we relate to others constantly flow through our subconscious, so when our identity is called into question by an organisation, even if we have learned over time to expect it, it inevitably produces a visceral reaction.

In psychology, this is called cognitive dissonance and defined as feeling stressed when we are required to do something contrary to our internal beliefs. It's such an important issue to consider when designing the security process that I considered *I Am Who I Say I Am* as an alternative title for this book.

Furthermore, while there is no doubt in our minds that we are who we claim to be, we also define ourselves by more personal characteristics, such as our name. When a security process requires us to define ourselves as a number, this causes an additional psychological disturbance, or even pain. We often subconsciously blame the organisation and the individual challenging our beliefs for this pain.

Perceived effort and risk

Success in getting through to the desired service is not the only measure of usability. The next aspect to consider is just how much effort the customer has to go through to achieve this. Effort in this context, while partially a question of time, which we will cover more when discussing efficiency in Chapter 3, refers to the mental and sometimes physical energy that the customer is required to exert to complete the process. This can range from low in the case of recalling their date of birth to far higher if they must find the card, the card reader and the PIN number they were sent several years ago that are now in a box in the attic.

There has been a lot of research into the relationship between customer effort, satisfaction and advocacy, which shows that minimising effort has a far greater impact than anything else on increasing customer advocacy.[1] This is true of the security process: though customers have been taught over many years to expect the process to be hard, they generally want the difficulty to be proportional to the perceived risk of the transaction and become dissatisfied when they consider their effort to be excessive.

Humans have always assessed risk relatively. I'm sure Stone Age hunters had a continuous internal dialogue about whether it was best to risk a maiming by a sabre-toothed tiger, dying of starvation or waiting for easier prey to come along. That's why when we call an organisation to ask its call-centre agent to do something, we have an innate perception of the risk associated with doing it.

Unfortunately, this assessment will not be the same for every customer because it is based on their prior experiences, knowledge and personal tolerance for the consequences of the organisation getting what they want wrong. Customers who have experienced significant detriment due to previous failings, such as a recent fraud or account compromise, will clearly have a different expectation to those who have little understanding of the risks. I'm not suggesting that this assessment is objectively correct, but in the mind of the customer it's perfectly valid.

The result of this assessment is that a caller's tolerance for the effort required to prove their identity will

1   M Dixon, N Toman and R DeLisi, *The Effortless Experience: Conquering the new battleground for customer loyalty* (Portfolio Penguin, 2013)

33

be relative to their own perceived risk of completing the task they're requesting. From an organisation's perspective, this risk and acceptable level of effort may vary widely from customer to customer, which is why it might sometimes be a good idea to allow customers to choose additional authentication requirements on top of those that you assess as necessary.

Cognitive load

Human memory and cognitive load have been studied for almost a century and the conclusions are clear: our memory is fallible. We are just not that good at remembering passwords and PINs. The longer we go without using them, the less likely we are to remember them,[2] and the more we must remember, the harder we find it.[3] This probably didn't matter when we had only one or two passwords, but now the average person needs to remember far more.

Based on data exposed in breaches, the most common PIN number in the world is '1234',[4] and the most common password is '123456'[5] – we

2   JA McGeoch, 'Forgetting and the law of disuse', *Psychological Review*, 39/4 (1932), p352, https://psycnet.apa.org/record/1932-04263-001, accessed November 2021

3   DR Pilar, A Jaeger, CFA Gomes and LM Stein, 'Passwords usage and human memory limitations: A survey across age and educational background', *PLoS ONE* 7/12 (2012), e51067, www.ncbi.nlm.nih. gov/pmc/articles/PMC3515440, accessed November 2021

4   'PIN analysis', *DataGenetics blog* (September 2012), www. datagenetics.com/blog/september32012, accessed November 2021

5   T Hunt, '86% of passwords are terrible (and other statistics)' (2 May 2018), www.troyhunt.com/86-of-passwords-are-terrible-and-other-statistics, accessed November 2021

understand our own fallibility and tend to choose things that are easy to remember. Most people recycle no more than seven passwords.[6]

Finally, it hurts when we're asked to do short-term manipulation of our memory. Figuring out characters two, five and eight of a twelve-character password is hard work.[7] It taxes our working memory, which only really has seven slots.[8] Is it any wonder that we can't always get it right and blame the organisation that sets the challenge rather than ourselves when we don't?

First impressions and trust

Researchers can't agree on how long it takes to form a first impression, but they can agree it is seconds, not hours. And once formed, it's tough to change; first impressions last for years, not days. Unfortunately, the security process is nearly always the first thing that callers experience when contacting an organisation, so it has a disproportionate impact on their first impressions.

---

6 D Florencio and C Herley, 'A large-scale study of web password habits', *Proceedings of the 16th International Conference on World Wide Web* (Association for Computing Machinery, 2007), pp657–666, https://rist.tech.cornell.edu/6431papers/FlorencioHerley2007.pdf, accessed November 2021

7 N Hogg, 'Measuring cognitive load'. In RA Reynolds, R Woods and JD Baker (eds) *Handbook of Research on Electronic Surveys and Measurements* (Hershey, 2007), pp188–194

8 GA Miller, 'The magical number seven, plus or minus two: Some limits on our capacity for processing information', *Psychological Review*, 63 (1956), pp81–97

The cognitive dissonance the customer experiences can easily translate into a feeling of not being trusted by an organisation they have selected to provide a service. Effort disproportionate to the customer's assessed risk of the task affects their perception of the organisation's competence. This perceived lack of trust and competence is amplified by the subtle signals they get from agents who are focused on 'getting through security' and carries through to how the customer feels about the whole experience. Even if the remainder of the interaction creates a favourable impression, when these initial feelings get reinforced through multiple interactions, they will have long-term implications on the customer's decision to continue doing business with the organisation or look for alternatives.

Customer effort

In their book *The Effortless Experience*,[9] Matthew Dixon, Nick Toman and Rick DeLisi of Gartner, a leading research company, explode the myth that loyalty is predicated on customer satisfaction and that customer delight is a cost-effective retention strategy. They show that the most effective strategy to mitigate disloyalty is to reduce customer effort in service interactions.

---

9   M Dixon, N Toman and R DeLisi, *The Effortless Experience: Conquering the new battleground for customer loyalty* (Portfolio Penguin, 2013)

In many cases, customers don't want these interactions at all, but when they do happen, their ongoing loyalty is influenced by how easy they perceive it is to do business with you. As a security process is required for nearly every service interaction, increasing its ease of use will have a greater return on investment (ROI) than any other service process.

Agent usability

The caller is not the only participant in the security process. Your frontline agents complete the process many more times, albeit with different pressures to get it right, so it has a significant impact on them as well. Asking the same questions on every call thirty to fifty times a day has a wearing effect on even the most enthusiastic agent. It is even worse if they don't believe those questions add much in terms of security yet feel the weight of responsibility to get it right, where 'right' is mostly defined as not letting fraudsters in rather than welcoming customers.

It's quite right that when fraud is identified, an investigation seeks to understand the root cause, but in many organisational cultures, this can seem to the agent involved like looking for a scapegoat. It's easy for them to be made to feel like they are to blame, even when it's most likely the process that failed them.

This impression is transmitted through interactions with team leaders and managers, and over time subtly changes everyone's attitude to the security process. Where once callers might have been given the benefit of the doubt, agents increasingly adhere to the process with a rigidity that is communicated to callers. The effect of this is twofold: on one hand, the caller is not made to feel welcome, and on the other, agents become obsessively focused on 'getting through security' before they even listen to what customers have to say.

The constant repetition of this 'us versus them' mindset where the caller must prove they are who they claim to be can have far-reaching consequences for the entire call-centre experience. It negates all the time, effort and money an organisation may have spent trying to create a customer-centric culture by reinforcing a company-centric culture and can turn agents into police rather than customer helpers.

Most frontline agents get job satisfaction from helping customers solve their problems, yet the security process risks them having to do the opposite: deny service to the customer. The key challenge is that most existing security processes give some form of discretion to agents. They are the ones who must determine whether what the customer is saying matches what the computer says or complies with the procedure. Even when the response is clearly wrong, the fact that the agent must make the decision puts the onus on them. When they must deny service, it can feel like it's their fault rather a failing of process, policy or data.

CASE STUDY: ACTIVE LISTENING

Most call-centre agents answer the phone with 'How can I help you?' or similar, but as we touched on earlier, many are more focused on 'getting through security' than listening to the customer. They often only hear a few key words and jump to a conclusion about the intent of the call before getting back to the security process.

I recently listened in to a customer call to an international bank. The agent heard 'South Africa' and 'Cash', so after struggling to get the customer through security, as he couldn't remember his PIN and hadn't updated his address in a long time, they launched into a transactional discussion on fees associated with automated teller machine withdrawals and how to order foreign currency.

The managers I was listening to the call with were dismayed that the agent didn't appear to have heard what the customer really said. If they had, then the conversation would have been very different.

The customer's son was travelling to South Africa for his gap year and needed a means to receive funds from the UK. For the bank, this could have meant a valuable referral to a partner bank and a customer who understood how they could transfer funds to that bank for free. The agent could have flagged up a range of travel insurance products and safety advice that might have been appropriate for the son (who was also a customer). Instead, the customer almost certainly left the call thinking his bank could do little for him and looking for an alternative.

For organisations seeking to build deep and lasting relationships with their customers, the long-term impact of the mismatch between the potential and the reality of this interaction could not be clearer. The agent's approach made the caller feel like a number, whereas if the agent had listened properly, they would have made him feel like a valued customer. Freed of the responsibility for making security decisions, the agent would have been able to focus fully on what the customer was saying.

Summary

Usability is the primary performance dimension of the security process. Wrapped up in human psychology, it's a complicated subject deeply linked to the behaviour of both customers and call-centre agents.

In this chapter, we've covered the key aspects of usability:

- If you can get usability right, everything else falls into place.

- The rate of FR is the key usability measure of process performance.

- Customers' overall experience of call-centre security arises from their perception of the balance between the effort they are required to put in and the degree of risk they feel exposed to.

- Without sound processes, agents may feel that they are always at risk of either denying genuine customers service or extending it to fraudsters.

- Processes that encourage agents to focus on listening to customers will enhance both customer experience and agent satisfaction.

3

Efficiency

Efficiency is often a proxy for the cost of the security process, but you need to consider more than the direct costs. In this chapter, we'll explore the expense of manual security processes and the missed opportunities for enabling self-service features that could obviate the need for an agent call altogether. We'll also discuss the often hidden overhead of knowledge-based security processes.

Handle time

The most obvious efficiency implication of the security process is the time your frontline agents spend completing it. While in theory, many identification and authentication practices can be completed quickly, the reality is often that they are not. Callers must go and find documents with reference numbers on them, systems are slow to bring up the relevant details, not every customer record has the information required, agents can't hear customers properly and must ask them to repeat things, and callers can't always remember the answers they need.

As a result, the average time spent on the process may be significantly more than you'd expect. When you include the time the agent spends explaining remediation processes to callers who can't complete the process, it can be longer still. In practice, the profile of time spent on security on your calls may be something like the curve shown in Figure 3.1.

When you consider that this pattern is likely to be repeated on many calls, it is not unusual to find situations where up to 20% of total talk time is spent on the security process. Just think what you could do if you got some of that time back.

Measuring average call security handle time

You may well be used to the concept of average handle time, but for the purpose of understanding the efficiency of different security processes, let's deconstruct the call a little further.

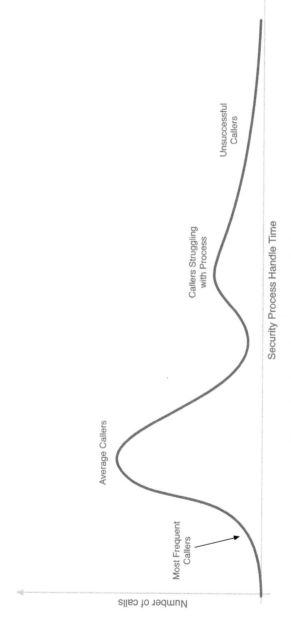

Figure 3.1: *Security-process handle time distribution*

Most calls follow a similar structure. An initial welcome and question about the customer's reason for calling is followed by the security process (made up of identification and authentication). The agent then attempts to resolve the customer's reason for calling and any additional needs before closing the call and completing after-call work.

When measuring the absolute time taken to complete a security process, we need to be careful that only this proportion of the call is counted. In some organisations, the only practical way to do this is with a stopwatch and an appropriately sized sample of call recordings.

Fortunately, many organisations have multiple identification and authentication methods, some of which don't require any agent time to handle because they are fully automated. Using these fully automated methods as a baseline, you can use the call talk time, which is usually recorded in the call-centre reporting suite, to compare the time taken for different security processes and outcomes. In most cases, the difference in time is almost entirely attributable to the different security processes.

Automation and self-service

The second element of efficiency to consider, and potentially the most significant, is the opportunity for self-service that the security process does or does not allow. Obviously, if a customer is seeking to do

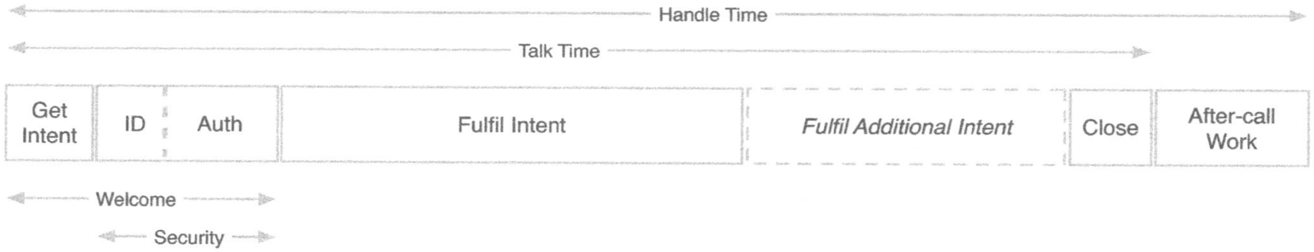

Figure 3.2: *Call talk time*

something themselves, wherever possible, we need to enable it and avoid the costs of an agent interaction, but in most cases, these services cannot be provided without identification and authentication. Once a caller has started speaking to an agent to complete the security process, there is little opportunity to return them to the increasingly capable range of voice-operated self-service solutions available.

To reduce handle time and exploit self-service capabilities, many organisations have automated some or all of the security process. But often, existing knowledge-based processes are hard to automate or require compromises to do so. In most cases, it is only possible to use simple questions or introduce PINs and passcodes, which have their own usability challenges. Even the best-performing organisations struggle to automate the security process in this way for more than 50% of their calls.

CAN YOU ENTER P@S5W0#D CORRECTLY ON A PHONE KEYPAD?

The context of use, including things like company logos and names, helps customers remember passwords and such.[10] It makes sense, therefore, to ask customers to remember one password to access all their services, otherwise it just makes the recall job harder. But if one

---

10 JS Nairne, 'The myth of the encoding-retrieval match', *Memory* 10/5–6 (2002), pp389–395, https://pubmed.ncbi.nlm.nih.gov/12396651, accessed November 2021

of the access channels is online, it really needs to be a complex password.

The theory of complex passwords – ones with upper- and lower-case letters, numbers and special characters – is sound: they exponentially increase the effort required by someone to guess them. Most password hackers use what are known as dictionary attacks where they try the most frequently occurring passwords first (based on those exposed in other data breaches), then the next and so on. You can find out if your password is included in these lists by checking it at https:// haveibeenpwned.com/Passwords.

Unfortunately, if one of the other access channels is a phone call, complex passwords will have a significant impact on the efficiency of the security process. Having introduced complex passwords online and in their telephone system, one large European retail bank found that the automated success rates for authentication almost halved overnight. This resulted in more calls needing to be authenticated by agents, which in turn led to more customers struggling to remember the details (probably because the context of use was different) and agents needing to use alternative and significantly longer methods to authenticate them.

Even if customers can successfully complete auto-mated processes many times, they often end up so worn out and frustrated that they are unlikely to fully engage with any self-service features available and prefer to speak to an agent. In this case, theoretically, there is some time saved as the agent should not need to complete the security process again and can get straight on with resolving the customer's reason for calling. Unfortunately, in practice, 67% of customers in research complained that they had to repeat their details again when speaking to an agent.[11]

There may be opportunities to shorten call time if, for instance, there is common or frequently requested information on every call, like minutes remaining for a mobile phone operator or the amount owed and due date for a credit-card company. Improving the rate of successful identification can have a significant impact on an organisation's ability to get routing decisions right first time and avoid the need for internal transfers. Identity adds important additional context to a caller's intent and can even help disambiguate between several reasons for calling, allowing customers at high risk of churn to be routed to a specialist team if their intent is related to a complaint or similar.

Cost of sustaining security processes

Many traditional security methods are expensive to set up and maintain. For a PIN to remain secret, it is often sent by post using special printing – a panel that needs to be scratched away to reveal the PIN when held up to the light – that prevents people from guessing what is in the letter or reading its contents without the

---

11 '5 trends in customer experience for 2020' (BT, 3 Feb 2020), www.globalservices.bt.com/en/insights/whitepapers/5-trends-in-customer-experience-for-2020, accessed November 2021

recipient noticing. While each letter may only cost a few pounds or dollars to protect, it soon adds up.

Some schemes attempt to increase the security of the PIN by requiring its receipt to be confirmed or it to be activated using another security method, which adds to the cost. During a typical customer lifecycle, it will not be unusual for them to forget the PIN at least once, and each occasion means another mailing.

When passwords are used instead of PINs, they too incur a cost to maintain as they add to the call length during setup, as well as when they are forgotten and need to be set up again. There may also be text messages, emails or letters to send to the customer to make sure it was they who requested the change, all of which have marginal costs.

When security processes involve high levels of employee discretion, you need to ensure that your agents are trained to make those decisions and check that they do so appropriately. Training and monitoring costs are difficult to avoid if you want to have confidence that your security process is performing as expected, but the more material cost in my experience is on employee morale and how that impacts absenteeism and sickness. Having removed employee discretion from most security decisions, one UK wealth manager attributed a fifteen-point increase in call-centre employee satisfaction, along with corresponding decreases in attrition and absence, to the change.

Agent of the future

Call centres emerged from the need to take orders and provide information to customers remotely. The agents in the first call centres were cogs in a machine because the technology to perform those functions didn't exist.

At the turn of this century, call centres were characterised as the workhouses of the new millennium by the popular press, but this is changing. Customers can now do far more for themselves online, and if they really want to phone in an order or to get information, the voice-driven technology that can accommodate them is a reality. When customers do speak to an agent, their needs are increasingly complex and often require emotional as well as functional input.

Nicola Millard, BT's chief futurologist, expects the role of the agent to change dramatically in the future, requiring greater empathy, problem-solving and technical skills than today.[12] These 'superagents' are unlikely to be the sort of people who are happy to spend a significant proportion of their day following a rigid security process. They are also likely to be a far more expensive resource, making it even less sensible for them to spend 10–20% of their time going through mechanistic security procedures.

---

12 NJ Millard, 'Botman vs superagent: Man vs machine in the future of customer experience' (BT, 13 April 2017), www.globalservices.bt.com/en/insights/whitepapers/man-vs-machine, accessed November 2021

Complaints

The final component of efficiency to consider is the cost of dealing with complaints related to your security processes, the failures of which are often a significant source of customer dissatisfaction. In many organisations, complaints must be handled in specific ways and may need to be reported to regulators. While many can be resolved with an apology and are rightly attributed to company policy rather than error, there is still a cost to receiving, investigating, responding to and reporting them that is often ten to twenty times greater than the cost of a single call.

Sometimes, the complaints don't even stem from the security process. I have seen examples of complaints or issues that only get formalised when a customer experiences security-process challenges or when restrictions in the security process prevent agents from resolving the issue to the customer's satisfaction. It's these frustrations that push customers over the edge; they've been prepared to tolerate the issue or problem up until this point, but when they are unable to access a service, are asked a question whose security value they perceive as limited or have to write in so that their signature can be verified, they finally crack, and all their frustration comes out.

CASE STUDY: PINS TO AUSTRALIA

Imagine the frustration of one customer of a UK bank based in Australia. Having accidently locked himself out of the online bank, he called a few days later to request a new passcode be sent to him. When the passcode arrived, he tried to use it, but it didn't work, so he phoned to ask for another one. He was reassured by the agent that one had already been sent, so was happy when it arrived a few days later, but not so happy when he was again unable to use it. After a few weeks of back and forth, and multiple replacements, he was still unable to access his account.

Unbeknown to him, a new PIN had been issued after he locked himself out of the online bank account. Because of the delay in receiving mail from the United Kingdom, when he called to request a new one, the process assumed the original had been lost. Unfortunately, from that point onwards, he was then stuck in a loop of always having the PIN number before the one the bank was looking for.

While this might be an extreme example, it does highlight the unexpected costs of maintaining these types of authentication methods, as well as the frustration they can create.

Summary

In this chapter, we have had a look at the elements of efficiency, including the expense of manual security processes. The key points covered are:

- Handle time and automation rates are the key measures of security-process efficiency.

- There can be hidden costs in maintaining knowledge-based authentication credentials.

- Frustration with security challenges can leave callers exasperated and unwilling to engage with self-service when they finally get through.

- Bad security-process experiences can exacerbate customer dissatisfaction, resulting in formal complaints and attrition.

4
Security

If security is the objective, then why does the security process so often fail to deliver it? In this chapter, we will explore fraudsters' methods and motivations so that we can design processes to counter them.

Success and failure

The simplest measure of the security provided by a call centre's identification and authentication process is the number of times it allows someone who isn't who they claim to be to access the service. We refer to this as a false accept (FA), because the objective of the process is to reject (true reject (TR)) callers who aren't who they claim to be.

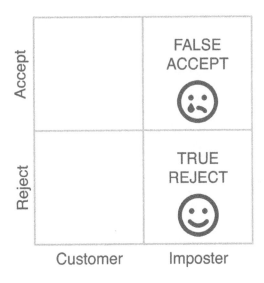

Figure 4.1: Imposter security-process outcomes

The problem is that when an FA does occur, it is unlikely to be immediately obvious. You may not find out for some time – or ever – so FAs are far harder to measure than FRs. Imposters' intentions vary: the purpose of the call may not be to compromise your call centre immediately, but to gather information to do so later, or even just to confirm some information they will use in another channel or against another organisation.

If nearly all calls are from legitimate customers, then there are obviously relatively few calls from imposters. The rate of imposter to genuine customer calls is known as the attack rate. Estimated attack rates vary widely by industry and language. In English-speaking markets, attack rates can range from 1 imposter for every 142 calls in retail through to 1 in 961 for retail banking, 1 in 2,199 for other financials and 1 in 7,143 or more for insurers and other low-value at-risk contexts.[13] Identifying them is like finding a needle in a haystack.

It's important to remember when referring to the FA rate for a security process that it is a function of the number of imposter attempts, not all calls. While a rate of 1% might sound high, it means that only 1 in 100 imposters was successful, not that 1 in 100 calls that passed the process were fraudulent.

Who and why?

Security in the modern call centre is, unfortunately, a battle between your organisation and imposters. Imposters will seek every opportunity to circumvent your systems and controls, so to defeat them, you must understand their objectives and motivations.

Organised criminals

Advances in technology have helped organisations be more productive and find new markets, but they have also done the same for criminals. Organised criminals often work in small groups or as individuals in loosely defined networks. Each participant may play

---

13 *Machine vs MACHINE: The battle for the IVR – Pindrop Voice Intelligence and Security Report 2021* (Pindrop, 2021), www.pindrop.com/pulse/reports/voice-intelligence-report-2021, accessed November 2021

a different role, but ultimately their objective is to access cash. Organisations with high-value products and those dealing in financial services are most at risk, but that doesn't mean that criminals won't exploit weaknesses in other organisations.

This group tends to be economically rational with an explicit cost (mostly time) and benefit calculation behind their decisions and a point at which it becomes too hard or not worth the effort to attack certain organisations and processes. At this point, they are likely to switch their attacks to other processes, channels or organisations.

Criminal groups are aware of many of the common means of detecting them and will attempt to co-ordinate and time their attacks to have the greatest chance of success. In many cases, they appear in waves as they seek to exploit a weakness before the organisation notices and closes it.

Opportunist

As anyone who has ever found a wallet with cash in it will know, there is a moment when we must decide whether to do the right thing and hand it in or take the cash and throw the wallet in the bin, knowing that no one will ever find out if we choose to do the wrong thing. Going further, what is the chance of getting caught if we try to use the cards and other information in the wallet?

While motivations vary from desperation to greed, the same moral dilemma exists on a wider basis. There is just so much information out there about individuals and many security processes are clearly weak, so the chances of success are high and getting caught low.

Individuals in the opportunist category lack the sophistication of more organised criminals, but because they usually only attack a handful of times, they can be harder to detect. In some cases, they may even be legitimate customers of your organisation who have found a way to exploit your processes for personal gain, such as receiving free or discounted services or repeated compensation for poor service.

Related parties

The final group that can be a significant source of security challenges contains individuals close to or related in some way to legitimate customers. The biggest challenge with this group is that in many cases, their intent is not malicious. They circumvent your controls to help friends or relatives who can't help themselves, often with the permission of the genuine customer, even if this is not formally recognised by your organisation. With many call centres, the caller pretends to be the customer rather than declaring who they really are.

Unfortunately, family relationships can be exploited, so every occasion on which someone pretending to be someone else accesses your services by compromising the security process is a failure. Most people know the key demographic details of others in their family and have easy access to incoming mail, devices and paper records. There are even cases where the genuine customer colludes with family members to embarrass and subsequently extort compensation from an organisation.

CASE STUDY: THINK LIKE THE BAD GUY

My last job before leaving the Army was to translate decades' worth of organisational experience from Northern Ireland in locating improvised explosive devices to train soldiers to do the same on the modern battlefields of Iraq and Afghanistan. Although soldiers had previously been taught specific procedures to counter the enemy threat, these procedures did not consider the wide variety of terrain in different countries and the continued evolution of terrorist capabilities.

Sun Tzu, the fifth-century BCE philosopher, general and writer, said, 'If you know the enemy and know yourself, you need not fear the result of a hundred battles. If you know yourself, but not the enemy, for every victory gained you will also suffer a defeat.'[14] Taking his comments to heart, I realised the key to adapting past experience for new situations was really understanding the aims and objectives of the

---

14 Sun Tzu, *The Art of War,* translated by John Minford (Penguin Classics, 2014)

terrorist at which point it became obvious how the environment and their available capabilities would influence their actions. One of the most successful exercises I designed to support this mental shift was for commanders to plan a terrorist attack on their own colleagues when they attended my training course. Only once they had been through the process of identifying options, selecting their preferred one and planning it in detail did I move on to training them to prevent it. Commanders trained to get inside the terrorists' heads and understand their intent were able to prevent the loss of many lives.

The same is true for your call centre. Understand your enemy well enough to anticipate their most likely forms of attack and develop countermeasures accordingly.

Fraud process steps

Of course, each failure of the call-centre security process is not necessarily a fraud; most fraudulent access attempts are just one step in a broader process. The most sophisticated fraudsters will move deliberately through all the steps shown in Figure 4.2 to achieve their objectives. Less sophisticated ones, while following a similar progression, will do so more loosely.

Figure 4.2: Fraud process steps

- **Acquisition** – in this step, the fraudster acquires partial or full information relating to a real person, their accounts or assets.

- **Reconnaissance** – the fraudster uses various means, often IVR systems and call centres, to understand more about their target, enriching the data they have with additional information such as how frequently the target accesses the service and the timing of large transactions. This enables them to plan and time the subsequent steps for maximum gain and minimal risk of detection. This reconnaissance step may also include small-scale tests designed to understand an organisation's processes and security measures.

- **Preparation** – the fraudster sets up the mechanism by which they will extract the goods, services or money. This can include changing delivery addresses or phone numbers so that goods are sent to a different location or notifications are not received, or adding new bank or beneficiary details to the target's account.

- **Extraction** – the point at which the loss occurs and the targeted organisation loses control of their own or their customer's assets. This may be choreographed in such a way that many attempts are made in a short period of time to maximise the return resulting from a new vulnerability, approach or data set, potentially overwhelming preventive measures.

- **Laundering** – in this step, fraudsters convert goods to cash, or transfer assets and cash in a way that makes their origin difficult or impossible to trace.

- **Access** – in this step, fraudsters are finally able to use the cash or assets for their own purposes.

Not all these steps have to take place in the same channel. An address may be changed in the phone channel before an item is ordered online.

Even if your organisation's goods and services are not the ultimate target of the fraudster doesn't mean it won't be involved in one of these steps. The information most organisations hold on their customers is valuable to fraudsters, especially given the human tendency to use passwords and memorable information across different organisations. Some service providers, such as email and phone companies, are also likely to be targeted because of the role their services play in securing other organisations.

Methods of attack

Through each step, fraudsters use a variety of methods to gain unauthorised access to information, goods and services.

Data loss and interception

There are many sources of initial data loss and exploring all of them is far beyond the scope of this book. They can range from simple mistakes, such as mail being sent to an out-of-date address or intercepted in a communal mailbox, through to far more sophisticated attacks that entail installing malware on a customer's machine or even a big business's website. There are also large-scale data breaches as a result of hacking. Fraudsters may take data from more than one of these sources to attack an organisation or its customers.

Automated validation and enrichment

The security process itself can be exploited by a fraudster to understand whether the stolen data is valid and useful. Automated systems can easily be set up to call an organisation's IVR system and enter information, the responses to this information revealing enough for the fraudster to tell whether it is valid or not. Similar processes are used with online portals, and other automated tools can match data from multiple breaches to identify potential passwords and other security information.

Customer social engineering

Often the final pieces of information the fraudsters need are in the hands of the real customers, so they exploit natural human behaviour to obtain this information. By creating feelings of distress, gratitude or urgency, they can get most people to provide the information they need to carry out their attack. While public awareness of this risk has increased significantly, for organised criminals, it is all about volume: they only need a few individuals to fall for their tactics to be successful overall.

Unfortunately, it's often the already vulnerable who are most liable to being exploited successfully, so lists of those who've been the victims of previous scams are regularly sold or passed on. Because the voice conveys emotion and builds rapport, phone calls (vishing) are the most effective form of this attack, but automated forms, including smishing (text messages) and phishing (email and online), have the advantage of scale. All use similar principles and are increasingly difficult, even for an expert, to distinguish from genuine communications.

Agent social engineering

There is another weak human link in the chain: an organisation's own agents. While your organisation will I'm sure have policies and procedures in place to prevent unauthorised access, it's often the agent who is the final decision maker. They decide whether to deny service or not and tend to be empowered to follow exception and override processes.

This means their natural human behaviour can be exploited as well. Even if they don't provide the caller with a service, they can still unwittingly provide information that may be helpful later. Fraudsters are master manipulators and agents are just as human as your customers.

Anatomy of a modern fraud attack

A cardholder's details (name, email, number, address, etc) have been compromised because of a data breach at an online shopping site. This information is sold on the dark web in batches by the initial digits of the card number, which identify the issuer. It's purchased by an individual who has experience in targeting a particular organisation and uses an automated dialler to call the bank's telephone helpline to confirm which cards are valid and still active (there is no honour among thieves – when they're selling lists of card numbers, they'll likely make a bit more money by adding some random numbers). Unfortunately for the fraudster, even when the numbers are valid, they don't have sufficient information about the customer to make a fraudulent transaction without compromising the card.

The details are sold on again to someone who calls customers about a suspicious transaction, pretending to be the bank's fraud department. Their fear of losing money and hope that the person calling can help them avoid this naturally reduces the customer's level of suspicion. When the caller says that they can stop the transaction, the customer is overwhelmed with gratitude and relief. The caller then says they are going to text an authorisation code to them and the customer thinks nothing of it.

Unbeknown to the customer, the fraudster is at that exact moment entering their details on to a retailer's website and triggering a text message security code as part of the payment approval process. When the customer reads back the code to the fraudster, they enter it and the order is approved. A brand-new laptop is on its way to the customer's address.

After hanging up, the fraudster immediately calls the retailer (spoofing their phone number so that it appears to be that of the customer). Sounding distressed, they claim that the laptop is a birthday present for their child at university, but now it won't arrive in time, so can they please change the delivery address? Because the caller can answer the security questions (which they set up when ordering the laptop), is calling from the number on the account and seems desperate, the retail associate goes slightly outside of policy and changes the address to that of one of the fraudster's accomplices.

Customer perception

While not impacting on real security, sometimes a customer's perception is just as important. When trust is essential in a relationship, customers need to feel secure. Sometimes this manifests itself as 'security theatre', such as the measures at many airports. While increasing the feeling of security, these measures do little or nothing to provide it.

As we discussed in Chapter 2, customers have learned over time to expect some degree of effort to get through security commensurate with their perception of the risk of the thing they are asking for. When this effort is absent, they can feel uneasy and unwilling to conduct business with your organisation, unless suitable reassurance is provided.

Summary

The third dimension of the security process is, fittingly enough, security. Whilst looking at the different aspects of security we covered the following key points:

- We need to get inside the minds of the fraudsters to design systems that will withstand them.

- The rate of FA is the key security measure of process performance.

- Fraudsters come in different guises, from organised criminals, through opportunists to parties related to the genuine customer.

- The fraud process follows a sequence of acquisition, reconnaissance, preparation, extraction, laundering and access. The call centre can be compromised in nearly all of these steps.

- Fraudsters' methods of attack vary according to their expertise and motivation.

- A customer's perception of security is as important as real security. No one is likely to want to do business with an organisation that makes them feel insecure.

5
Tradition And Transition

The methods and processes we use to secure our call centres today have evolved over time as the environment we operate in and the technology available has changed. In this chapter, we'll explore the challenges of these methods and the approaches that lie behind their adoption and use.

Security approaches

Most call centres today approach security in one of three ways:

Traditional security

With this approach, organisations focus on securing the 'front door' of their call centre using knowledge-based authentication questions relating to information the customer has provided during onboarding or throughout their relationship with the company. This internally focused approach will typically use reference and account numbers to identify customers.

I refer to this approach as traditional because until recently, it was the only one feasible for many organisations seeking to serve customers remotely.

Transitional security

Recognising the challenges of knowledge-based authentication, many organisations attempt to combat the security and/or efficiency weaknesses by introducing additional authentication methods, such as OTPs or substituting questions for PINs and password challenges. I refer to this approach as transitional because while it addresses short-term concerns, it is not sustainable in the long run.

To improve efficiency, organisations adopting this approach may well use a variety of identification methods to increase automation. While secure, these methods often have other weaknesses, as well as a detrimental impact on customer usability. When fraudsters discover and exploit these weaknesses, organisations have nowhere else to go, so they have to focus on increasing detection measures rather than preventive security.

Modern security

This book recommends a philosophy and approach to securing your call centre that I refer to as modern security. As a philosophy, it seeks to use advances in technology to maximise the usability and efficiency of the process while delivering the required level of security. It recognises that no one method or combination will meet all customer or organisational requirements, and that both technology and the fraudster threat will continue to evolve. At its heart, it aims to maintain an appropriate balance between each dimension of performance for its context of use.

We will cover the modern security approach and methods in Chapter 6.

Traditional and transitional authentication methods

At the heart of every security process is at least one authentication method. While every security process is dependent on identification, it is the authentication method that has the most significant impact on the overall usability, efficiency and security of the process.

Question bank

You are probably familiar with this process, which uses demographic information about the customer (name, address, date of birth, mother's maiden name, etc) and/or relationship information (details likely to be known only to the organisation and customer, such as current balance, recent transactions and products held). Typically, agents ask between two and four questions from a set, depending on the availability of the data, and follow specific rules about how many answers the caller can get wrong before being denied service.

As we discussed in Chapter 4, the prevalence of data loss and human susceptibility to social engineering mean that this method isn't particularly secure. In many organisations, it continues to play a role as 'security theatre' when the likelihood of imposters attempting to access is small and the consequences negligible.

As the threat increases, the natural tendency is to add questions and increase the obscurity of the answers the call-centre agents seek. Initially just time consuming, this approach can soon become unusable for a significant proportion of callers who can't remember the information they are supposed to. This approach is also hard to automate in a voice or push-button self-service application because of the wide range of possible responses.

The major advantage of this approach is that the information required is already part of the customer's record, so can be implemented and changed with little extra effort. While customers may be frustrated by these questions, they tend to see the failure to provide the correct answer as their own fault, so the organisation escapes blame.

SECURITY THEATRE BECOMES SECURITY FARCE

The phrase 'security theatre' was coined by Bruce Schneier in his book *Beyond Fear*,[15] published two years after the terrorist attacks in the United States in September 2001. His contention is that security is both logical and instinctual: you can calculate it, but you also need to feel it.

Security theatre emerges as a response to people feeling insecure, even when purely objectively, they are safe. Measures that can be construed as security theatre include troops deployed on the streets following major terrorist events (often without rounds in their weapons) and tamper-evident seals on medicines. In practice, they don't increase the objective and measurable risk of attack or poisoning, but they do have value because they make individuals feel safe enough to resume normal behaviour or purchase the item.

In security theatre, at least one party and usually both believe the process adds security value, and it's just the

---

15 B Schneier, *Beyond Fear: Thinking sensibly about security in an uncertain world* (Copernicus, 2003)

decision makers who know it doesn't really. Knowledge-based questions in the call centre are different. In this case, agents know the process doesn't stop fraudsters and callers know it's not adding security value. It's only the decision makers – the organisations – that believe it does add security.

PINs and passwords

PINs and passwords emerged to streamline and improve the security and efficiency of authentication processes, but they are still knowledge based. The security improvement is a result of the secret information being known only to the organisation and the customer, but this requires some effort to establish. Provided the customer remembers the secret information, they can be optimised for use in an automated system, or at least to reduce the amount of time an agent needs, thus improving efficiency.

The downside is that this secret information is easy to steal from overhearing or interception, and for this reason, additional measures are needed to protect it. These range from disguised envelopes and an expensive printing mechanism that makes it difficult to read PINs when they are sent out, to the practice of the customer only giving certain letters or digits when speaking to an employee, so that no employee ever hears or sees the full PIN or password.

PINs are significantly easier than other knowledge-based methods to automate using a phone's key pad, but passwords that incorporate special characters can be challenging. From a customer perspective, if either is used frequently, it becomes easier to use, but as the frequency of use reduces, so does the ease. Because customers often use the same passwords or PINs with multiple organisations, they are reasonably easy to elicit by fraudulent means and can be compromised in data breaches outside an organisation.

Origins of the PIN

While passwords have been widely used by the military for centuries – you can trace their origins back through history to ancient civilisation – the PIN is a far more modern invention. In 1967, Barclays Bank introduced the first cash machine at its branch in Enfield Town, using specially encoded cheques rather than plastic cards. For the first time, customers had to enter a PIN to gain access to their money.

Within a few short years, PIN use was ubiquitous and deeply ingrained in the public psyche.

SMS one-time passcode

As a result of the almost universal adoption of mobile phones, many organisations have started to use text messages as an authentication method. By sending a unique code to the known phone number of a customer and asking them to repeat this to an agent or automated system, an organisation can be more confident the caller is who they claim to be.

This is a form of possession-based authentication because it assumes that if the caller has the correct code, they are in possession of the customer's mobile device. It makes a lot of sense because most of us would be quick to identify the loss of one of the objects most central to modern life.

The downside is that it can be challenging to use in a call-centre context because there may be a delay in the message being received. Then there are usability challenges with relaying a number from a device that is also being used to make the call. For this reason, OTPs are often used as an additional authentication method rather than the primary one.

Unfortunately, there are weaknesses in both the phone network and mobile phone operators' own security processes that make it relatively easy to redirect these messages. Text messages are sent to phone numbers, not devices, and phone numbers are owned by the phone company. Such companies make it easy to move an account to a different device, and this can be exploited by fraudsters. Furthermore, at no point in transit across the phone company networks is a text message encrypted, so any relaying party can see its content. Finally, there are opportunities for customers themselves to be socially engineered into giving these codes to the wrong person.

Hardware-based possession methods

These methods employ devices that typically generate an apparently random number every thirty or sixty seconds and display it on a screen. Sometimes, the device is standalone, and sometimes it requires a bank or smart card with a chip to be inserted. In practice, each token (usually the card) has a unique seed value known to the issuing organisation that can be used to calculate which number should appear.

A card reader combines both knowledge (of the PIN) and possession (of the card) in a single package. Because the response is numeric, it is easy to automate, making it an efficient and secure form of authentication. Even without the PIN, hardware-based authenticators provide significant security, but are less likely than a phone or card to be missed if stolen. Furthermore, a systems breach can expose all a manufacturer's seed values.

Hardware-based authentication is generally expensive to establish because of all the devices required, along with the need to post them and often confirm receipt with the customer. From a customer's perspective, it can be convenient, but they do have to have the device on them, which makes this method more useful in business-to-business (B2B) interactions where users are likely to be in the same location when remote authentication is needed. A consumer customer may not be at home, or even remember where they have stored the device.

Mobile app-based methods

As the sophistication of mobile devices increases, organisations are developing their own apps. This is mostly to support customer self-service, but they can also play a role in call-centre security.

Mobile apps can provide a far more secure communications channel than SMS, as in-app messaging is significantly less vulnerable. They can be used to generate OTPs without the need for additional hardware and even secure the phone call itself. When they press a click-to-call button, additional security information can be provided to a call centre to confirm the caller's identity.

All of these points take advantage of the customer's device's own security features, which may include fingerprint and facial biometrics, and confidence in ongoing possession by the customer. Even without this secure calling approach, mobile app-based methods can significantly improve the efficiency of a call centre using them.

These methods can be secure if implemented correctly, but some are vulnerable to social engineering, and all are dependent on the device's own security features being set up appropriately, both of which are beyond the control of the organisation. Critically, they are dependent on the customer installing the relevant app and setting it up, so they may be of limited use for organisations that can't persuade their customers to do this.

Active (text-dependent) voice biometrics

Voice biometrics or speaker recognition is the statistical comparison of a caller's speech pattern with a previously recorded version. The combination of physical characteristics (such as length of vocal tract and chest size) and behavioural characteristics (such as accent and language) that influence these features means that everyone's voice (as with a fingerprint) is unique to them.

Text-dependent verification requires the speaker to say the same thing as they did on the original recording. The process of establishing this recording is known as enrolment and usually requires the customer to repeat a phrase such as 'My voice is my password' multiple times. As everyone's voice is unique, this comparison can produce high levels of security, although the fact that the customer always says the same thing does make it vulnerable to presentation attacks, in which a recording of the customer's utterance is replayed to the system.

As the authentication process can be completed in the IVR system, it can support increases in automation and enhance efficiency. But while voice biometrics has high levels of usability because of the customer not having to remember any information or access devices, the artificial repetition of a phrase in the enrolment and authentication process does inhibit the number of customers willing to use it.

To summarise, let's compare the pros and cons of each method.

Table 5.1: *Comparing traditional and transitional security methods*

Method	Advantages	Disadvantages
Question bank	Simple – based on existing customer and transaction data	Security – many data points may be shared between organisations or available in the public domain
PIN and password	Efficiency – can be more easily automated than question bank and usually requires fewer questions	Security – open to social engineering Cost – expensive to establish and provision
SMS OTP	Easy – the majority of customers have mobile phones, so this method doesn't require anything to be installed	Usability – can be difficult to locate and enter while using the same mobile device to make the call Security – increasing range of techniques to intercept or divert messages

Method	Advantages	Disadvantages
Hardware-based possession	Secure – especially when combined with a knowledge-based factor to mitigate risk of loss	Possession – hardware token needs to be with customer whenever they want to make a call

Cost – expense of issuing and maintaining hardware tokens |
| Mobile-app based | Secure – as long as customer has provisioned mobile app and uses it

Easy – visual interface enables smoother process | Usability – can be difficult to use while making the call on the same device

Coverage – requires customer to install and use mobile app |
| Active voice biometrics | Easy – customer doesn't have to remember anything

Efficient – can be easily automated

Secure – unlikely to incorrectly accept imposter | Usability – requires customer to enrol and repeat fixed passphrase

Security – vulnerable to replay and presentation attacks |

Summary

Call-centre authentication has evolved over time, but many of the methods we are familiar with have been in use for decades. In this chapter, we have looked at the most common authentication methods, comparing and contrasting what each one can offer in terms of usability, efficiency and security.

We covered the following key points:

- Traditional methods focus on securing an organisation's 'front door'.

- Transitional security methods seek to tackle the weaknesses of traditional methods by introducing additional challenges.

- All authentication methods have advantages and disadvantages, many of them dependent on the attitudes and abilities of customers.

- Modern security achieves the most effective balance between usability, efficiency and security.

PART TWO

MODERN CALL-CENTRE SECURITY

Moving on from traditional and transitional approaches doesn't mean throwing everything away. While the modern security approach introduces some new methods, it's the philosophy and process behind it that will deliver the most significant benefits and truly unlock your call centre.

This section is about understanding exactly how your process performs today, the constraints of your organisational context and how to shape your modern security process while gaining the support you need to implement it.

6

Introducing Modern Security

Modern call-centre security is both a philosophy and a practical approach. In this chapter, I will introduce the principles in more depth, along with a range of technologies that enable them to be delivered.

Principles of modern security

The modern approach employs advances in technology to maximise the usability and efficiency of the process while delivering the required level of security. It is not prescriptive, but based on five principles:

- **Minimise friction** – the easier security processes and methods are to use, the more likely customers are to adopt them and adhere to them. The quicker they are, the more efficient they will be for frontline colleagues.

- **Prefer authentication** – the more confident we can be that someone is who they claim to be, the less we need to worry about FAs. Detective measures can complement, but never replace strong authentication.

- **Strengthen with depth** – as a call progresses and understanding of its relative risk increases, there are opportunities to implement additional authentication and detection methods. It doesn't all have to happen at the front door.

- **Adapt to risk** – not every call has the same risk profile, so not every call needs the same security treatment. Variation is acceptable.

- **Select for flexibility** – new vulnerabilities and risks will emerge, so security methods need to be flexible and capable of change over time without compromising the other principles.

A modern security process is likely to use one or more advanced technologies that display properties consistent with the principles. These methods need to be:

- **Passive** – requiring little or no effort from the customer to complete authentication, reflecting the principle of minimising friction.

- **Dual purpose** – usable for authentication if possible or detection if not, reflecting the principles of preferring authentication and adapting to risk.

- **Probabilistic** – returning results that reflect the probability of the caller being the customer they claim to be or an imposter. Allowing varying levels of confidence for different requirements reflects the principles of adapting to risk and flexibility.

- **Continuous** – usable at different stages of the call, increasing confidence over time and reflecting the principle of strengthening with depth.

Passive (text-independent) voice biometrics

While active (text-dependent) voice biometrics has been used in IVR systems with some success since the turn of the millennium, it is only more recently that advances in computing power, machine learning and digitisation of underlying call-centre platforms have made it feasible to use voice biometrics alongside agent calls without the customer being required to say the same thing every time.

The key difference between active and passive is that in the latter, both enrolment and authentication take place without the customer or agent having to do anything they would not otherwise have to do to resolve the issue on the call. Typically, a customer is enrolled during a conversation with an agent, and when they call back, an authentication result is available after a few seconds of normal conversational speech.

This authentication method provides a score reflecting the degree of confidence that the speaker is the customer they claim to be. It requires identification in advance of authentication, but it can use all the audio gathered during the call to return a result as soon as the identification is confirmed.

The accuracy of text-independent voice-biometric technology continues to improve as the length of audio needed for both enrolment and authentication and identification reduces. As a result, it is now feasible to use this technology with the brief utterances typically given by customers in speech-driven IVR systems, particularly if they encourage more conversational dialogue, such as those with natural language understanding (NLU).

Text-independent voice biometrics can also operate in an identification mode. This is most often used as a fraud-detection tool to check whether a speaker claiming to be a customer who is not enrolled for authentication sounds like a known fraudster. In this mode, the system compares the features extracted with those of a group of imposters and returns a score as to how likely the caller is to be one or more speakers in this group.

In addition to this watch-list capability, some voice-biometric systems are able to compare large samples of calls and identify those on which the speaker sounds similar, even when they are claiming to be different customers. In this way, they can identify fraudsters who have not previously been flagged for inclusion on a watch list. Similar techniques can be used to assess other customer attributes, such as age and language, to provide additional data points for comparison with the customer's record or previous calls.

Network authentication and detection

These methods use signalling data from a phone call either to confirm that the call originated from a device known to be in the possession of the customer (authentication) or to detect when the call has originated from a device, location or network indicative of suspicious behaviour (detection).

We are all now used to the calling party's number appearing on our phone, but many of us are probably not aware that as the call is routed between different parts of the phone network, there is a significant amount of additional data attached to it that can be interpreted to determine where it came from and what route it took. If this is combined with insight into known suspicious or authentic activity, it is possible to decide as to the relative risk of the call.

As well as that which is attached to the call itself, information is available from network providers and carriers about the status of a subscriber's device and account. This can provide further indications as to the risk that the caller is not who they claim to be.

At the simplest level, this technology compares the inbound automatic number identifier (ANI) or caller line identifier (CLI) representing the caller's phone number with your customer records. If you want to use the phone number as a form of possession-based authentication, though, you need to mitigate the risk that it, or the device, is no longer in the possession of the real customer or has been maliciously manipulated (spoofed). In the case of mobile phones, it is often possible to identify the device by its unique identification number, which is independent of the phone number assigned by the network so a truer test of possession.

Even when the number presented is not associated with a known customer, it is possible to use the same data points to assess the likelihood that the caller is a fraudster. While a caller's telephone number may be withheld or easily changed, if similar signalling data is associated with multiple calls claiming to be from different unrelated customers, then it is highly likely that fraudsters are attempting to gain unauthorised access. Similarly, if the data indicates that the call originates from a network known to be favoured by fraudsters, perhaps because its security processes are weak, then it would rightly attract more suspicion than a call from a domestic landline associated with the customer's geographic location.

Number spoofing

Just because the number on your caller display says that your mother is calling doesn't mean that she really is. Unfortunately, the technology and protocols that underpin the global telephone network were designed when there were relatively few operators and they could all be trusted to follow the rules. Now, the sheer number of telephone service providers and the myriad of interconnections between them make this trust and standards-based system vulnerable to manipulation, as the plethora of unwanted calls and messages we tend to receive every day attests.

The ANI or CLI received on your device cannot be trusted to belong to the originating subscriber because it is the network's responsibility to advertise the number associated with the call. As there is no central registry of assigned numbers, any network with an interconnect to another network can advertise a number they don't technically own. There are many apps/services available specifically to spoof number information that use this anomaly.

Behavioural analytics

This is the third modern security method. It covers a broad category of technologies that can evaluate both the contents of a call and how it progresses in relation to what you would expect from a specific customer, customers in general and/or imposters.

In just one call, there may be many data points available, such as the speed, duration and spacing of key presses in an IVR system, the words the caller uses to introduce themselves or request certain services, the day of the week and time of day of the call, the size, type and destination of the customer order, and the history of recent logins to the organisation's online service. In some cases, data points like this are sufficient and distinctive enough for you to be confident that the caller is the customer they claim to be (authentication), but in most call centres, there are far fewer data points available than there might be for similar techniques in mobile or online apps. Call centres are more likely to use this as a detection method to increase agent confidence that the call is genuine and not fraudulent.

In the detection cases, relatively few data points can yield significant results. For example, preventing fraudsters using an automated system via IVR to confirm customer details can often be as easy as identifying the inhuman regularity of its keypresses compared to those of a typical customer. At a more complex level, this mode of detection could go as far as assessing customers' transaction requests as in or out of character, or suspiciously like other recent requests by other customers that were suspected to be fraudulent. This is known as transaction screening and is commonly used across all channels, not just the call centre.

As behavioural analytics systems have evolved, they have taken on two distinct forms. The simpler forms are rules based with logic statements to the effect that if x is observed, then carry out task y (often restricting or denying service). As more and more rules are added, the complexity – and the management over-heads – increase significantly.

The alternative is to provide as many data input points as possible to a 'black box' system using artificial intelligence and machine learning, giving sufficient feedback on whether calls were fraudu-lent or not for the system to learn to predict the status of future calls. But it can be difficult to understand the black box system's decisions and it's impossible to train it for situations that haven't happened yet.

Let's compare the pros and cons of each modern secu-rity method.

Table 6.1: Modern methods comparison

	Advantages	Disadvantages
Passive voice biometrics	Accuracy – the principal advantage of voice biometrics is its high level of accuracy Low customer effort – passive in authentication and detection, requiring minimal effort to register	Registration – requires the customer to be enrolled in advance of authentication Consent – biometric data often needs the customer's consent to process, which increases customer effort and time during registration
Network authentication and detection	No customer effort – in both authentication and detection, this method requires no effort from the consumer	Related parties – it is feasible for parties related to the customer to gain access to their device with malicious intent Data dependent – requires that the number or device is registered in advance of authentication
Behavioural analytics	Simplicity – can use data and simple rules in your existing line-of-business systems No customer effort	Lower accuracy – because of the limited data points available, this method is unlikely to be viable for many authentication cases without investment in additional data points, such as speech-to-text analysis

Understanding the performance of modern methods

One of the key differences between traditional and modern security methods is how they derive their outcomes. From a business process perspective, the outcome usually needs to be a true or false response. Either the caller is who they claim to be or not.

Traditional methods are deterministic in that a caller either passes or fails the process. In other words, they get the PIN number right or they don't. There is no middle ground. Modern methods are probabilistic: they return a score which reflects the probability that someone is who they claim to be or, in a detection role, that a certain characteristic is present. This is then converted to a pass-or-fail decision by way of a threshold score (a score that must be reached or exceeded).

As we discussed in Part One, there is a risk that both modern and traditional methods will lead to the wrong outcome. During authentication, the genuine customer may be rejected (FR) or an imposter accepted (FA). During detection, suspicious activity may be missed or innocent activity incorrectly alarmed.

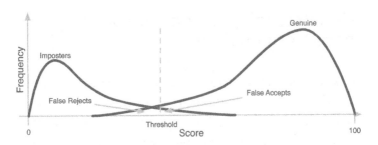

Figure 6.1: Genuine and imposter outcomes

The crucial difference is that with modern methods, you can calibrate the threshold score to an appropriate position for your organisation. Figure 6.1 is an exaggerated graphical representation of this. In a score range of 0–100, genuine customers will tend to score in the upper range and imposters will tend to score in the lower range, but for a variety of reasons (which depend on the method), occasionally some genuine customers will score poorly and some imposters highly. The position of the threshold score is therefore the key determinant in the number of FRs and FAs, represented by the area underneath the respective curves on opposite sides of the threshold. This holds true across all forms of modern authentication, even though their scoring processes may be less granular.

We will examine how to establish the threshold in Chapter 14. For your call-centre security's planning and design process, it is essential to recognise that reject outcomes are inevitable, and it is more likely than not that they will happen to genuine customers.

Delivering modern security

Designing modern security for your call centre and transitioning to it requires a considered process which reflects the current situation and addresses its key challenges within the constraints of your organisation. These process steps form the basis for the remainder of this book.

1. **Understand current performance** – ensure you understand how your existing security process performs in terms of usability, efficiency and security to identify the priorities for improvement and articulate the opportunities.

2. **Understand context** – understand the constraints and opportunities created by both your customers' behaviour and your organisational environment.

3. **Plan methods and mix** – identify the optimal method or methods of improving security-process performance.

4. **Make the case for change** – develop and communicate the business and emotional case for change to relevant stakeholders.

5. **Implement** – design and implement the specific business processes and technology required to support modern security.

6. **Optimise** – measure and manage the process to deliver optimal outcomes.

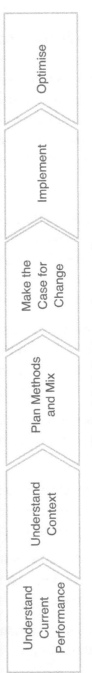

Figure 6.2: *Delivering modern security*

Summary

In this chapter, we have looked at the principles of modern security and the technologies that enable them to be delivered. We have also looked at the differences between traditional/transitional and modern security methods, along with the process for designing and adopting modern methods.

The key topics we explored are:

- Modern security processes make it easier for customers to access services, increasing efficiency while strengthening security.

- Modern methods of security are passive, dual purpose, probabilistic and continuous.

- Passive voice biometrics enables customers to be authenticated during a normal conversation.

- Network authentication and detection use signalling data from a phone call to confirm or reject an identity claim.

- Behavioural analytics draws on multiple data points to establish whether a call conforms to the customer's established pattern of behaviour.

7

Understanding Current Performance

Before setting out on any long journey, we need to know where we are starting from. In this chapter, I will introduce my key tool for understanding the performance of a security process, the Security Path Visualisation. This will give you a clear baseline on which to build your modern security processes and metrics that will track improvement over time.

Security Path Visualisation

In Part One, we established the key performance dimensions of the security process, but we now need to understand how your current process performs against them in sufficient detail to identify opportunities for improvement. This would be simple if all callers took a single path through the process, but of course, they don't. There are many possible outcomes.

The Security Path Visualisation will help you understand and communicate the different paths your callers take. As well as this, it shows the proportion of callers taking each path, which can then be assessed for its usability, efficiency and security performance. Depending on the proportion of callers using it, each path can be weighted to understand the aggregate performance of your entire process.

In the worked example, used throughout this chapter, there are only two outcomes from each identification and authentication step – 100% of calls start on the left, and then pass through different steps before achieving one of seven outcomes. These outcomes range from never speaking to an agent because their needs are resolved in self-service through to failing to complete the security process successfully because of not being correctly identified. Each of these outcomes has a different usability, efficiency and security profile.

To build your own Security Path Visualisation, there are four steps:

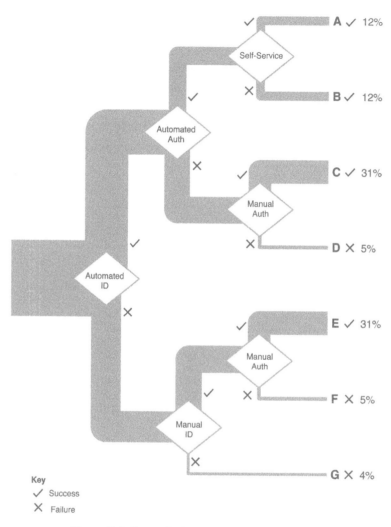

Key
✓ Success
✗ Failure

Figure 7.1: *Example Security Path Visualisation*

1. **Identify the key decision points** – these are usually automated identification, automated authentication, manual identification, manual authentication and self-service containment. Some organisations may not have automated methods or self-service, and some may bypass decision points, depending on the caller's intent, so you may need to remove or add additional decision points accordingly (see Figure 7.2).

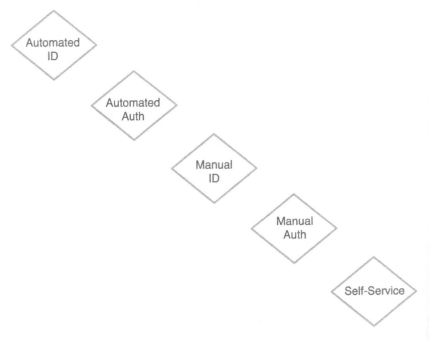

Figure 7.2: Identify decision points

2. **Identify the paths and outcomes** – there should be at least two paths from each decision point, reflecting success or failure at that point (see Figure 7.3). Some organisations may have different levels of confidence from a decision point reflecting different authentication methods (for example, some may allow limited information to be given to callers who can only answer one or two questions), which should be represented as different paths.

For ease of reference, it is helpful to label each path and whether the outcome is success or failure from the perspective of the customer. You might also consider colour coding the final path with red for failure, green for success and amber for anything else.

3. **Evaluate the number of callers passing down each path** – this can be the hardest step as the information may be spread across different systems. While it would be ideal to know how many callers passed down each path, it's often difficult to know which callers were identified by manual means (and how) and which by automated means.

Although these are two separate paths, it may be necessary to assume initially the same ratio of passes to fails at each similar decision point. In comparing the numbers produced by different systems, you may also see disparities caused by unexpected behaviour, such as callers who fail automated identification hanging up before connecting to an agent for manual identification. In these cases, it may be appropriate to add additional paths.

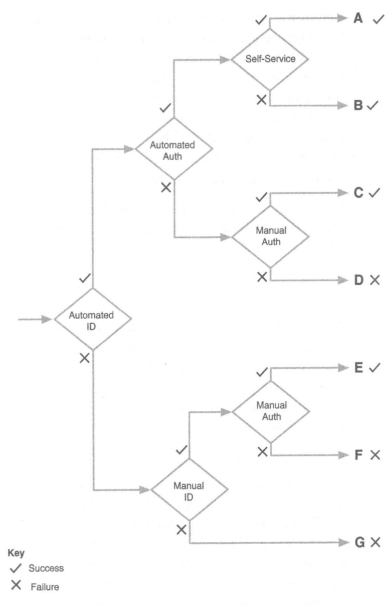

Figure 7.3: *Identify paths and outcomes*

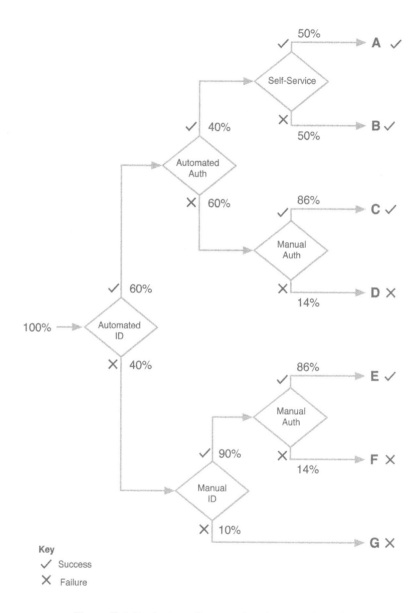

Figure 7.4: *Evaluate callers passing down each path*

In Figure 7.4, I have used percentages instead of absolute numbers for simplicity.

4. **Calculate key statistics** – the key output of the Security Path Visualisation process is the number of callers receiving each outcome (on the far right) and the percentage of total calls they represent. For example, the proportion of calls talking path E is the product of the nodes these calls pass through in Figure 7.4 (ie 40% × 90% × 86% = 31%). Each of these outcomes is also quite different from the perspective of usability, efficiency and security. Changing the thickness of each line on the chart makes it far easier to understand how callers are flowing through your security process.

It is helpful to aggregate these outcomes into some summary statistics showing usability and efficiency outcomes:

- Callers failing to complete security process
  = D + F + G

- Callers requiring manual identification
  = E + F + G

- Callers requiring manual authentication
  = C + D + E + F

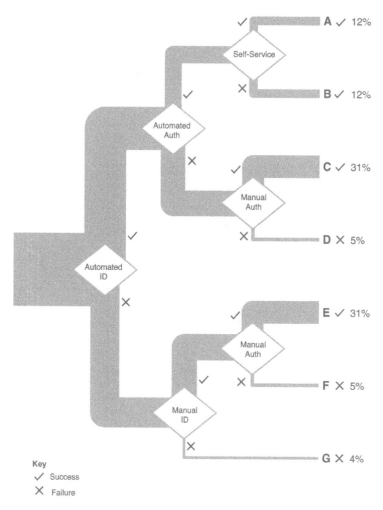

Figure 7.5: *Calculate callers taking each path and outcome*

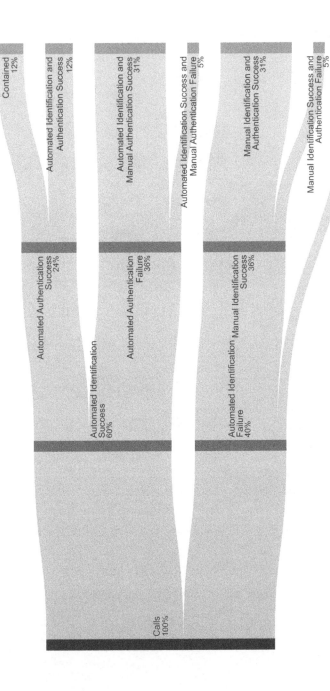

Figure 7.6: Example Security Path Visualisation using Sankey diagram

There are many ways to draw this graphic with specialist tools or in simple PowerPoint diagrams, but it is essential to use thickness of the paths as a visual signpost to the number of callers taking each one. Over the years, I have found this to be by far the most powerful communication tool when trying to increase stakeholder understanding of the existing challenges. You can download templates or use my online tool to produce Sankey diagrams that highlight the flow volumes at www.symnexconsulting. com/unlock-book.

CASE STUDY: WHAT IS THE REAL CHALLENGE?

The Security Path Visualisation process, which I have developed with clients over several years, has time and again proved itself to be the critical step in strategy development. It has led to many revelations for clients, such as:

- An investment manager discovered that despite improvements in their automated authentication process, it was the low proportion of customers they were able to identify automatically that was preventing them realising the efficiency benefits of new authentication methods.

- A retail bank realised that if it wanted to improve the security of its call centre, it needed to prioritise automated authentication processes over agent ones as most of its existing callers already used this process.

- Another client saw that while they could identify most callers before they spoke to an agent, their biggest challenge was high drop-out from their automated authentication process.

Measuring usability

You can quantify the usability of your security process by looking at two related areas:

- **FRs** – The Security Path Visualisation provides the proportion or number of callers who are incorrectly rejected (FRs) through the sum of the 'fail to identify and/or authenticate' paths. As we assume that nearly all callers are who they claim to be or have a legitimate desire to access our services, these must be considered service failures.

- **Customer effort** – while most callers will complete the security process successfully, the degree of usability in their experiences may differ widely. You can understand the relative effort and the impact of different paths on overall effort by assigning a usability score (as a percentage) to each identification and authentication method. I have provided examples of scores used in my online scorecard tool in the callout boxes below, but consider amending these scores to reflect your unique circumstances. The paths' aggregate usability is the usability of each of the methods multiplied by one another (ie identification method usability × authentication method usability) except where the path results in a failure outcome, when the usability should be scored as zero. You can then use the proportion of callers on each path to weight these scores against each other to obtain an overall score.

Overall usability score = ((Path A proportion of callers) × (Path A usability score)) + ((Path B proportion of callers) × (Path B usability score)) + ...

The quantitative approach is useful for comparison between organisations and over time. It can highlight particularly challenging experiences, but it doesn't reflect the real impact of poor usability on customers and agents. To complete the picture, look at the consequences of poor usability:

* **Customer dissatisfaction and attrition** – there are several different ways of assessing customer satisfaction with your existing security processes, which may also identify additional benefits from a better process. If your organisation has an active post-call customer feedback programme, you can use the results of these surveys to compare the relative satisfaction of customers who took different paths. You could also consider bespoke surveys to question customers on issues related to the security process, such as their perceived effort and the appropriateness of the methods. Finally, it's likely that some customers who are rejected incorrectly will be so dissatisfied with their experience that they complain or even terminate their relationship with the organisation, so review the difference in complaint and attrition rates

between those who were successful and those who were not.

- **Agent dissatisfaction** – your frontline agents can provide feedback on the usability of the existing processes and their frustrations. A key driver of overall employee satisfaction relates to the tools and processes available to them, so this information is usually already captured in organisation-wide employee surveys.

  It may be helpful to go beyond this and establish a specific survey of the relevant agent groups, focusing on satisfaction with the security process. You can ask how agents' degree of satisfaction has affected their likelihood of staying in their role or organisation unit. Agent focus groups can also be used to gain further qualitative and anecdotal evidence of challenges with existing processes, as well as customers' reactions to them. These qualitative measures are difficult to attribute to individual paths, but they nonetheless provide important supporting evidence for the current state of the security process.

Identification methods' usability

In my scorecard, I use a scale of 0–100% to quantify the usability of different identification methods in five categories:

Organisation-issued identifiers are the account and reference numbers generated and issued to customers. The baseline usability score of 50% assumes that these are numeric, contain no more than eight digits and are readily available, such as on regular statements or other communications. If the identifier is more obscure or complex (perhaps containing letters as well as numbers), it is likely to be harder to remember and use correctly, so warrants a lower score.

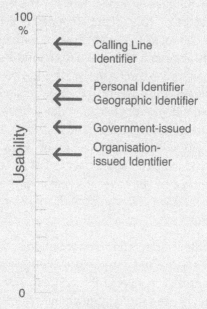

Figure 7.7: *Identification method baseline usability scores*

Government-issued identifiers are references such as National Insurance or Social Security numbers.

The baseline usability score of 60% reflects that customers use these numbers frequently, so they are easier to remember, tempered by the fact that callers are possibly reluctant to share them because of the security implications, even though they are only for identification in this context. If these types of identifiers are not frequently used in your country or are long and complex, a lower score may be appropriate.

Geographic or location identifiers are references such as an address or phone number. The baseline usability score of 70% reflects that nearly every customer will recall their own address with ease, but as this approach often requires multiple steps, such as confirming the postal or zip code before the first line of the address, it is more challenging to automate. If your organisation does not regularly use mail to contact its customers and there is a risk that your address data may not be up to date, consider reducing this score because of the extra effort required by the caller to remember the address they gave you when the relationship was established.

Personal identifiers refer to information such as the customer's name and date of birth, which should never (or rarely) change. In this context, date of birth is being used for identification rather than for authentication, which is how most organisations currently use it. The baseline score of 75% reflects the easy ability to recall, mitigated by the multiple steps likely to be needed in its use.

CLI or ANI doesn't require the caller to do anything because it uses their incoming telephone number to compare with your records. The baseline usability score is 90%, reflecting the lack of effort in this method. This is tempered by the fact that a proportion of callers will share the same number, so the agent will need some form of disambiguation.

If your organisation uses only mobile numbers, because these will apply to fewer callers overall, they may warrant a higher score. Calls initiated from your own mobile apps or websites, where the customer identity is passed to you, could be categorised similarly, depending on the effort required in the app itself.

Measuring efficiency

You can quantify the efficiency of your security process by looking at two dimensions.

Security-process handle time

This is the amount of time spent by agents on the process. The handle time for each path can be calculated using the average time for each step, recorded using a stopwatch or by categorising calls according to their path, and calculating the difference in talk time between them. Using the process handle times and the proportion of handled calls for each path (excluding calls that were handled by self-service and therefore didn't connect to an agent), you can calculate the average security handle time and compare this with your average handle time (AHT) to understand the percentage of all available time that is attributable to the security process:

Average security handle time = ((Proportion of handled calls on Path A) × (Security handle time Path A)) + ((Proportion of handled calls on Path B) × (Security handle time Path B))

For example, in Table 7.1:

(13.6% * 0) + (35.2% × 52) + (5.7% × 76) + (35.2% × 65) + (5.7% × 96) + (4.5% × 75) = 54.4 secs

Proportion of all available time spent on security processes = Average security handle time / Average overall handle time

For example, in Table 7.1:

54.4 secs / 312 secs = 17.4%

This number is often higher than people expect; it can vary between 5 and 25% of all talk time. You can append the security handle time and proportion of security handle time for each path to the visualisation in Figure 7.5 to make comparisons between the proportion of callers on each path and the relative handle time to identify disparities (eg Path F = 10% of security time but only 6% of callers). You can download a spreadsheet to help you with these calculations from www.symnexconsulting.com/unlock-book.

Table 7.1: Example security path handle times
(not all calculations shown)

Security path (Figure 7.5)	Proportion of all calls	Proportion of handled calls	Average handle time	Security-process handle time	Proportion of security handle time
A	12%		0	0 secs	0%
B	12%	13.6%	300 secs	0 secs	0%
C	31%	35.2%	352 secs	52 secs	33.6%
D	5%	5.7%	376 secs	76 secs	8%
E	31%	35.2%	365 secs	65 secs	42%
F	5%	5.7%	396 secs	96 secs	10.1%
G	4%	4.5%	375 secs	75 secs	6.3%
Average[16]			312 secs	54 secs	17.4%

Self-service enablement

Calls that never reach an agent will not require any agent handle time, so represent significant avoided effort. As most self-service is not possible without the caller successfully completing the automated security process, this value needs to be represented in

---

16 The averages in this table are weighted based on the proportion of calls taking each path. You can download a spreadsheet from my website www.symnexconsulting.com/unlock-book to help you with these calculations.

our assessment. The proportion of all callers whose needs are met by self-service (Path A in our example) of those who completed automated identification and authentication (Path A + Path B in our example) is the key metric. In our example, it is 50% – ie 12% / (12% + 12%).

Measuring security

When you're quantifying the security performance of your process, the primary measure must always be the rate of FAs. If possible, annotate each path with the percentage of FAs and the total value of any loss that they represent.

Unfortunately, this can be hard to measure for a variety of reasons. Incidents of FA are rarely obvious when they occur and are dependent on their ultimate consequences being attributed to the interaction. If an organisation's own goods and services are not the ultimate target of fraudsters, many incidents of security failure may go unreported. In some industries (particularly B2B or where family members look after the affairs of others), it is common practice for callers to share passwords and other authentication information. As this doesn't result in a reportable fraud or loss, it is not counted either. Even attributing a value to each path may understate the real level of incidence or do so in a biased way.

As with usability, I have developed a scoring model for the security of each authentication method, which you can use to assess your current process. I assign a score to each different path, and then use the proportion of callers on each path to weight these scores against one another to obtain a weighted average and overall score.

Overall security score = ((Path A proportion of callers) × (Path A security score)) + ((Path B proportion of callers) × (Path B security score)) + …

Authentication methods' usability and security

In my scorecard, I use a scale of 0–100% to quantify the usability and security of different authentication methods and group them according to whether they are knowledge, possession or inherence based, as described in Chapter 1.

- **Knowledge-based methods** are typically fairly usable, depending on the complexities of provisioning and recall, but provide limited security as they can be easily socially engineered. Baseline scores in this group range from personal information, with a usability of 75% and security of 20%, to PINs, with a usability of 40% and security of 50%.

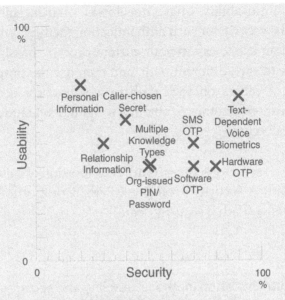

***Figure 7.8**: Authentication method
usability and security*

- The usability and security of **possession-based methods** vary quite widely. They are typically more secure than knowledge-based authentication, but less usable because of the effort required to establish them. Baseline scores in this group range from SMS OTP, with a usability of 50% and security of 70% (assuming suitable safeguards are in use), to hardware OTP generators, with a usability of 40% and security of 80%.

- **Inherence-based methods** are generally both secure and usable, but depending on the type chosen, they require some effort to establish.

The baseline score for text-dependent voice biometrics is a usability of 70% and security of 90%.

To use this model in your own organisation, determine how many examples of each method you have, and then make assessments as to their relative security and usability before assigning a score between 0 and 100% to each.

To help you understand the current state of your security process, I've developed a simple online calculator enabling you to make an initial assessment of its performance. You can find it at www.symnexconsulting.com/unlock-book. The calculator will provide you with a score (out of 100) for each of usability, efficiency and security, and generate a simplified version of the Security Path Visualisation. The process takes no more than ten minutes to complete, and you can then use the output to understand if a more detailed assessment is worthwhile.

Summary

In this chapter, we have introduced the Security Path Visualisation. This tool gives you a clear baseline on which to build your modern security processes and metrics that will track improvement over time.

The key points we've covered are:

- The starting point for introducing modern security is an assessment of your organisation's current performance.

- Building a Security Path Visualisation for your process will help you understand the variation in performance across every permutation and combination of your customers' experience.

- The usability of your process is measured by the number/rate of FRs, the degree of customer effort along with agent and customer dissatisfaction, and rates of attrition.

- The efficiency of your process is measured through handle time and the degree of self-service enablement.

- The security of your process is measured through the rate of FAs and fraud incidents.

You can use the scorecard at www.symnexconsulting. com/unlock-book and the additional measures of usability and security above to help with your assessment.

8

Understanding Context

The security process does not exist in a vacuum. What works for one organisation in one sector or market may or may not work for yours, depending on your organisational context. In this chapter, we'll explore the two key determinants of that context: customer behaviour and transaction risk.

Before we start, though, there's one important thing to remember at all times:

We are not like our callers.

I have been guilty of making this mistake more times than I care to admit, so I want to reiterate why we aren't, so that you don't make the same mistakes when designing your security process.

- We do this all day, every day – we think about phone calls, how callers get from A to B and the processes they are subjected to. Our customers just want their problem solved.

- We understand the consequences – we know how the bad guys operate and clean up the mess when they are successful. Our customers just want their problem solved.

- We understand the product – we know how it's supposed to operate, how to get things done, what is a real issue and what isn't. Our customers just want their problem solved.

- We understand our competitors – we probably have a good feel for when their proposition or service is better or worse than ours. Our customers just want their problem solved.

Let's now have a look at the things to keep in mind when you're developing your modern call-centre security process in the context of your organisation and industry.

Customer attitudes and behaviour

It goes without saying that your customers are not all alike, so you need to consider what differences in their attitudes and behaviour are likely to impact the design of your security processes. One aspect of this is their attitude to automation – their willingness to engage with it or do things themselves.

The availability of other self-service channels, like online or mobile, will influence their willingness to use automated security processes, stay within a self-service application or do everything manually with an agent. It will affect the likely complexity of their needs when they call, and therefore your ability to solve their problem through self-service features rather than an agent.

Another aspect of customer behaviour is the degree of trust they have in you, which is influenced by whether they have any choice in accessing your services. Callers can access your services in many different capacities beyond that of consumer: as an employee of another organisation; as a taxpayer or citizen with no choice but to contact you; as a patient dependent on your services. These roles, along with the type of goods or services your organisation delivers, will influence their expectations of security and usability, as well as the degree of trust they have in you.

Evaluating caller behaviour and attitudes to the security process is subjective. To bring customers to life and test decisions about the optimal security mix, I recommend you develop a handful of personas that represent the diversity and breadth of your caller population. At least this will stop you making the mistake of treating everyone as a clone of you and ensure that your design supports a range of customer needs.

The example personas coming up provide a good basis to start from for most organisations where they don't already exist, but I advise you to enrich them with your own insights. Given opportunity and time, frontline agents are best placed to describe the different types of callers they encounter daily, and you can then group them based on the key attributes you identify.

Meet the customers

These are deliberately extreme descriptions (archetypes) designed to highlight the contrasting attitudes and behaviours found in typical callers:

- **Connie Convenience Seeker** – Connie just wants to get the job done. She hasn't got time to think too deeply and chooses to use the telephone because it is convenient to her at the time, so her needs may not be that complex. She will follow the path of least resistance and effort and try her best with traditional security approaches, but she may struggle if she doesn't have the information to hand.

- **Andy Automation Rejecter** – Andy refuses to engage with any form of automation and just wants to speak to a real human being. He gets easily frustrated by passwords and PINs and doesn't trust the computer to get it right; if he can remember his PIN or password, he certainly won't be providing it to an automated system. He prefers to build relationships with individuals.

As a result, he doesn't use many online services and often calls for reasonably simple needs.

- **Do-it-myself Dave** – Dave is Andy's opposite: he'd far rather do things himself than ask for help. He does most things online, so if he calls for help, he's probably exhausted all options and his needs will be relatively complex. He doesn't use the phone channel often so won't remember channel-specific security requirements, and while he will try to use them, he will quickly get frustrated if the automated experience is not well thought out.

- **Power-user Pauline** – Pauline is an engaged customer, and her primary service channel is the phone, which means she calls frequently and knows her way around the telephone system and processes. She knows exactly what to expect at each stage, so is well prepared and often gets straight to the point. Her needs are not usually complex and she doesn't struggle with traditional security measures, but can get frustrated when things change.

- **Disengaged Derek** – Derek may never have called before because he had forgotten about this product or service, and has only now remembered because he's encountered a problem. He probably doesn't know much about the product or understand its features and is unlikely to have any recollection of any information he provided your organisation, or you provided him.

Caller frequency

The security process is based on individuals, not calls. The same individuals will tend to act in the same way, no matter how many times they call, and most modern authentication processes need to get to know the customer before they can be effective. Caller frequency, therefore, has a significant impact on the appropriateness and effectiveness of different methods.

Many call centres already report an average number of calls per customer, but these aggregate numbers can mask what is really happening, leading to false assumptions about the future. Wherever possible, get underneath these numbers and understand the distribution of caller frequency across a twelve-month period. I have seen cases where more than 60% of calls come from the top 20% of callers.

From this analysis, you should be able to understand how many callers made two or more calls in the twelve-month period. As many modern authentication methods require enrolment in a prior call before they can be used, this is an important determinant of likely in-year benefits. Organisational data going back further than twelve months is usually more difficult to obtain, but if you can do so and estimate the number of contacts in a customer's lifetime, it can help make a compelling case for improving the security process.

As an alternative, if the data is not available, you can review your call mix from the perspective of your product and customer relationship. I generally see four types of calling pattern:

- **Transactional** – customers are purchasing a product or service that has few ongoing needs. They largely call to purchase, and if they do call subsequently, it's about a problem with initial provisioning. Average calls per customer may be fewer than two per lifetime.

- **Enabling** – you provide a product or service that is critical to the customer's day-to-day life, such as banking or telecoms. The complexity and centrality of these services to the customer's life tend to increase demands, typically driving an average call per customer of more than two (often much more) spread out over the period of the service. If churn rates are low, their relationship with your organisation can span many years.

- **Case based** – customers call with a specific issue or transaction requirement that is likely to need several contacts in a short period of time, such as purchasing a property or claiming against an insurance policy. Average calls per customer are often three or more, all of which happen over a short period of time.

- **Periodic** – you provide a product or service that is mostly forgotten by the customer, apart from on some form of periodic cycle, such as investment products at tax year end or insurance at renewal time. Average calls per customer per year may be fewer than two, but if the product is long lived, they will call consistently year after year.

Many organisations will have a mix of these caller types. An insurance customer may call once a year to haggle about a renewal until they need to make a claim, when they might call several times. This exercise is nonetheless useful to help you understand the most appropriate security methods and how long it might take customers to feel the difference from changes you make to the security process.

Transaction risk

Most calls entail some risk to an organisation, but that risk will not be the same on every call. To determine the appropriate mix of security methods, you need to understand the relative risk of each call.

By understanding the customer's reason for calling on each occasion and the services that were provided, you can determine the level of risk from their calls. I use this hierarchy to categorise calls, but you may find that you need to modify this slightly:

- **No risk** – these calls are usually generic information requests such as store or branch opening hours and returns policies, so there is no requirement to know the customer's identity before providing the information.

- **Disclosure risk** – these calls elicit some indication that the claimed identity is a customer of your organisation, but no more. This category may include parts of your security process that vary depending on whether the identity is recognised. Most calls are likely to fall into this category or a higher one.

- **Information risk** – in these calls, the customer is supplied with additional information about the products or services they have with you, which could include personal information. This can range from providing a balance or an order summary through to detailed investment breakdowns. Most calls fall into this category.

- **Indirect loss risk** – in these calls, the agent is asked to supply information or a service that may compromise your security process, allowing a direct loss later or in another channel. Customer requests in this category typically include things like changing a name, address or contact details on an account or customer record.

- **Direct loss risk** – these calls could result in you losing control of customer or company assets and resources or compromising other elements of your security. Customer requests in this category typically include purchases and payments.

Consider whether the goods and services your organisation provides have the potential to compromise elements of another organisation's security, for example provisioning a SIM or providing a customer's date of birth. This might not be a direct issue for you, but there are likely to be long-term reputational consequences of enabling fraud elsewhere.

Your organisation's reputation is arguably its most valuable asset, and a significant part of reputation is trust. If, as a result of security-process failures, customers don't trust you to do the right things, the longer-term financial impact, though harder to quantify, can be far more significant than any direct loss.

Understanding the mix of risk on your calls is essential to knowing what appropriate security looks like. It may be that more than 80% of your calls fall into the first three categories, or it may be that the majority are in the last two. Each has different implications for what appropriate security means.

Summary

What works for one organisation's security processes may not work for yours, depending on your organisational context. In this chapter, we've explored the two key determinants of that context: customer behaviour and transaction risk. These are the factors that shape how you design your security processes.

The main points we explored are:

- Customer behaviour varies widely, but most callers fall into one of several broad categories.

- Caller frequency information is essential to assess the appropriateness of different modern methods.

- Risk can also be divided into broad categories, according to the type of information the caller is requesting.

- Different types of call represent different degrees of risk. Even those that may seem low risk in terms of your assets may compromise your reputation.

9

Planning And Mixing Methods

You now have a good understanding of how your current security process performs (Chapter 7) and the organisational and customer context (Chapter 8) that might constrain your ability to improve it. In this chapter, I'll introduce a framework for your modern security process and explore how you can select the right methods and elements for your organisation. This framework is intended as a way of thinking rather than a prescriptive solution. Every organisation is different, and the right answer for each will be too.

There are undoubtedly opportunities to improve the performance of your security process by making better use of existing methods. This approach can deliver some short-term value for relatively little cost, but over time, it is likely to prolong or even increase imbalances in security-process performance. For example:

- Automating knowledge-based authentication might improve organisational efficiency, but it is likely to frustrate customers further and introduce additional security vulnerabilities that can be exploited by fraudsters in the future.

- Optimising traditional or transitional methods by increasing the use of more secure steps such as SMS OTPs will undoubtedly improve security, but at a significant cost to both customer experience and efficiency.

- Introducing transitional methods can improve security and sometimes efficiency, but may increase customer effort significantly.

As a short-term solution to address critical issues, you may have to start here, but I encourage you to initiate the process of designing a modern security experience so that you can evaluate the full benefits for your organisation.

Plan your modern security experience

Reflecting the principles of minimising friction, preferring authentication, strengthening with depth, adapting to risk and selecting for flexibility, there are up to eight components in a modern security process. There must be primary and fallback methods of identification and authentication with optional detection. There may also be a requirement for step-up authentication and detection methods. These components are represented graphically in Figure 9.1.

Figure 9.1: Modern security process matrix

When you're planning the process, consider:

- **Primary identification and authentication methods** – these should be appropriate for most of your callers and calls.

- **Fallback methods** – these methods will be needed for when the primary method is unsuccessful, such as in the case of an FR or when the customer is not set up. They are likely to be based on existing processes.

- **Detection methods** – because every modern method can also be used in a fraud-detection capacity, even if authentication is not possible, the same technology can often assess the risk of fraud on the call.

- **Step-up methods** – additional methods may be required if some calls have a significantly different level of risk associated with them.

Not all callers will be able to take the path of least friction, but you should aim to maximise the number that do.

Strengthen with depth

Defence in depth has been a key tenet of military strategy for more than 2,000 years, with the first recorded use by Hannibal in 216 BCE.[17] More recently, the strategy has been adopted by security professionals to protect networks and information systems.

In the call centre, traditional security often takes a single line of defence. I refer to this as 'front door security', where if the caller gets through the initial security process, they can do anything they like with few if any further checks. This leads to the challenges we discussed in Part One: to prevent imposters,

---

17 M Phifer, *A Handbook of Military Strategy and Tactics* (Vij Books India, 2012)

organisations try to make the front door as secure as possible, to the detriment of both usability and efficiency.

A modern security process recognises that most callers don't want to do anything significantly risky, so it uses a defence in depth approach to ensure that the degree of security is appropriate to the risk the caller and call pose. I break calls into five phases, each of which provides an opportunity to add an additional layer to the security process.

Figure 9.2: *Available layers of defence in a call*

In each of these phases, you can deploy both positive authentication capabilities, to increase confidence that the caller is who they claim to be, and negative detection capabilities, to increase confidence that the caller is not an imposter. Most organisations will not need to use all these opportunities, instead selecting the most appropriate.

Table 9.1: *Layers of defence examples*

	Authentication	Detection
Start of call	To have sufficient confidence to confirm the caller is a customer and support most servicing requests	Based on the incoming call's characteristics
Initial	To have sufficient confidence to confirm the caller is a customer and support most servicing requests	Based on additional features obtained during the authentication process
Mid	Additional steps (step up) depending on the nature of the service requested	Based on characteristics of call, caller and request
End	Additional steps (step up) depending on the specific risk of the order, transaction or service	Based on the specific details of the order, transaction or service
Post-call	Post-call or out-of-band confirmations from legitimate customer required to allow the transaction	Allowing legitimate customers to repudiate requests, changes and transactions

Primary identification and authentication methods

In keeping with our principles of modern security, the primary identification method should be passive, requiring little or no customer effort. In most cases, this means using the incoming phone number as the identifier. We will cover this and the use of other phone network data for both identification and authentication in Chapter 13.

The primary authentication method is the preferred method for every call and, as the new front door of your organisation, should exemplify the principals of modern security. To maximise the opportunities for automation, it needs to return a result quickly and with minimal customer effort. Therefore, it is likely to be a choice between network authentication and voice biometrics, both of which provide good levels of security with minimal customer effort for authentication.

While voice biometrics provides higher security as it authenticates the individual uniquely, it does require extra effort to register the customer, so is not appropriate in every case. Network authentication only authenticates possession of a device, so it is dependent on that device being used to call and still being in the possession of the customer. I recommend selecting the method based on the frequency of calls and level of risk associated with the majority of calls.

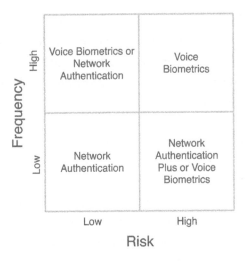

Figure 9.3: Selecting primary authentication method

When the caller frequency is relatively high (ie more than once per year), then I recommend voice biometrics as the primary authentication mechanism. This allows for the caller to register on the first call, and you'll both receive a return on this time and effort investment within a relatively short period.

Where there is low risk in a typical call, network authentication is also a viable method, but not preferred. In this quadrant, determining the optimal method for your organisation is likely to depend on:

- **Longevity** – whether the authenticated device is likely to continue to be used, the customer relationship is likely to be lasting and / or the risk profile may change in the future

- **Related party risk** – if a related party may incorrectly authenticate as the customer by using the same device or line

- **Perception** – if customers need to feel 'secure' to have confidence in the organisation, the service or advice provided – in which case, more visible or effortful methods may be required

Where caller frequency is low, network authentication is likely to be the primary authentication method if you have a record of your customers' numbers. Where the transaction risk is high, particularly when the risk may come from parties related to the customer, you will need to supplement this method with an additional authentication or detection method to provide an appropriate level of security. Depending on the risk, this could be implemented as a step up rather than an initial authentication step.

If the relationship between the organisation and the customer is going to last for many years, it may be better to use voice biometrics as the primary authentication method, particularly if there is a long time between contacts and a consequent risk of device information and customer records becoming outdated. It is, of course, possible and potentially even desirable to combine both methods to get maximum caller coverage and security.

Primary detection measures

As not all callers will be able to use the primary method your organisation has chosen, because they are either not set up or not calling from a recognised device, there is opportunity to use the authentication method or an alternative in a detection role before, during or after initial authentication. Even if the incoming number is not recognised, network detection capabilities will be able to identify if it is coming from a high-risk destination or shows other signs of suspicious behaviour.

Voice-biometrics capabilities can be used to identify frequent imposters from watch lists or when the same individual is claiming multiple identities, although both functions tend to require more audio than might be obtained during initial authentication so are better deployed as in-call measures. It may be possible to implement behavioural detection capabilities early in the call to confirm that the caller is not a bot attempting to gain information from your IVR system or using known fraudster tactics to compromise your security processes.

Fallback identification and authentication methods

When the primary method or methods are unable to authenticate the caller because they are not enrolled, the data is not available or they have been rejected, then a fallback is required. In most cases, this will be your existing authentication process, but if the customer is enrolled to use the primary method, this failure of authentication needs to be considered when you're deciding what transactions and services you'll provide access to. The most likely path for an imposter to take is to fail the primary method and use the fallback method.

The longer customers have been using a new method of security, the lower the chance that they will remember their PIN/password when they need it. In most cases, a simple knowledge-based question process, subject to enhanced fraud-detection measures, should allow them access to a restricted level of services.

Step up

Although you select a primary authentication method that provides confidence for most calls, there may still be cases where the initial authentication outcome is not adequate for the risk in the service or transaction the caller requests or where detection capabilities have flagged up a reason for heightened suspicion. In such a case, you may want to implement step-up authentication using a method different from the original:

Table 9.2: Step-up authentication options matrix

Original	Primary step up	Secondary step up
Network authentication	Voice biometrics	Knowledge
Knowledge-based questions	Possession-based authentication	Additional knowledge-based questions
Voice biometrics	Network authentication	Knowledge

Step up is most useful in cases where you're employing network authentication and the particular transaction has a high risk from parties related to the registered customer. Here, you may need to use alternative methods to confirm that you are speaking to the genuine customer. Unfortunately, if the call is from an imposter, they already have access to the device, and possibly to the customer's other communications channels such as their email account, since they have passed the initial authentication, so other forms of possession authentication are ruled out in this situation.

End-of-call authentication and detection measures

As the call ends, there is far more information available about the specific transaction, allowing you to decide whether to allow the transaction, allow it with some additional authentication, or deny it. If your security processes have achieved sufficient confidence, you can allow the transaction, but if not, consider whether notifications or transaction screening will provide adequate detection measures for mitigating the risk.

These approaches are only relevant where it is possible to build in some delay to allow the customer to repudiate the transaction or for a system or analyst to review it in detail. If this is not possible or if transaction screening is unable to release the transaction, then you may require an outbound authentication request. Ideally, this uses the primary authentication mechanism to confirm the customer's identity before the details of the transaction are confirmed and it is released.

Notifications as a detection method

While organisations often write to their customers about different aspects of the products and services they provide, they may overlook the security value of these notifications. In many cases, they provide a cheap and easy way to offer a genuine customer the chance to repudiate a call or transaction.

Repudiation is the denial of the truth or validity of something. In the context of modern security, it creates an opportunity for genuine customers to reject fraudulent requests and transactions, which has a valuable strengthening effect. Notifications are usually sent to customers via an alternative channel to the one through which the request was made, such as email or text message. In my experience, customers are generally quick to respond in cases where the request is not genuine, often taking only a few minutes to do so, depending on the delivery channel.

In this way, notifications can be an incredibly cost-effective method of adding additional confidence to business decisions. Your organisation may already have the infrastructure in place to send text, email and in-app messages at minimal cost. These types of notifications have the advantage of the genuine customer receiving them shortly after the reported transaction, adding extra security to transactions that have natural delays in processing, such as order fulfilment and trade execution.

In some cases, it may even be appropriate to build short delays into otherwise instantaneous processes to allow for notifications to be received and responded to. They add little friction to the genuine customer as they tend to be ignored at worst and welcomed as extra reassurance at best.

Letters sent by traditional mail can also provide an effective opportunity for customer repudiation. While less vulnerable to technical compromise, they will, of course, take longer to arrive and may be intercepted. They are more appropriate to provide an opportunity for customers to repudiate changes to their records, such as address, contact details or enrolment status, where the impact will be felt over a longer time.

Orchestration

There are many interrelated components and decisions in a modern security process, so to manage it effectively, you need some form of process orchestration tool. While this can be purchased from a supplier, it can also be developed as a set of rules and decisions in your business applications. A simple hierarchy and scoring system is usually all you require:

- **Authentication success** – add points for the strength of the authentication methods (eg voice-biometrics authentication = 20pts).

- **Detection alarm** – subtract points from the authentication score relative to the confidence in the detection method (eg network detection alarm – not from normal devices -5pts, so total = 15pts).

- **Transaction risk** – evaluate the risk of the transaction/service requested based on its characteristics (eg check status of order = 5pts).

- **Step up if applicable** – if the score for a call is less than the transaction risk, prompt the agent to complete additional authentication steps (5 < 15, so there's no step up required in our example).

- **Determine outcome** – if the score is greater than or equal to the transaction risk, allow the transaction. Otherwise, deny service or follow exception process for post-call authentication/ review (15 > 5, so in our example, the request can be completed).

The complexity of this process will clearly increase as additional security methods are introduced and the transaction risk is reassessed, but the basic framework is simple enough for everyone to understand.

Summary

You need to begin planning your modern security experience by selecting primary identification and authentication methods while accepting that not all customers will be able to use them. For this reason, ensure that you have appropriate detection, fallback and step-up methods in place.

The key points we covered in this chapter are:

- A customer's incoming number delivers the best modern identification process.

- Select the appropriate modern authentication method according to caller frequency and transaction risk.

- Remember there's strength in depth. The use of step-up, fallback and post-call authentication and notification elements adds depth to your overall security process.

- A framework for orchestrating your security process will deliver the best outcome for every customer.

10

Making The Case

Once you've planned your new security process, you will need to persuade stakeholders across your organisation to provide you with the time, resources and support to implement it. In this chapter, I will show you how to make the case effectively in a way that supports your stakeholders' rational and emotional decision making.

The rational side will require some form of business case that estimates the costs and benefits of the changes you want to make. But in most organisations, there is no shortage of business cases that show a positive ROI; to secure support, you will also need to persuade stakeholders through an emotional case. The rational case tells the story in numbers, but the emotional case tells it in feelings. What will it feel like when your proposed changes are implemented? What might it feel like if they are not? Both cases are important and need to be developed in parallel.

The key challenge in making the case for modern security is that it benefits customer experience, cost efficiency and security. Because of this, it touches many different business functions, each on its own probably not being compelling enough for stakeholders to prioritise the required improvement.

Business case – benefits

While the areas in which modern security delivers benefits are clear, estimating their financial impact and the timing of this impact can be challenging. You will need to consider:

- **Efficiency** – the most significant cost benefit area is likely to be reducing the number of calls that need to be handled by agents through enabling more automation and / or cutting call length by removing the requirement for agents to complete the security process. There may be further cost savings from reduced investigation requirements, lower costs of provisioning traditional authentication material such as PINs, and the potential to cut the costs of hiring and onboarding agents through lower attrition.

- **Security** – reducing the number of fraud incidents also reduces the resultant financial loss. Some organisations treat the cost of fraud as contingent rather than budgeting for it. Because it is significantly influenced by changes outside the organisation, it can be difficult to quantify benefits here.

- **Revenue** – increasing customers' satisfaction will lead to reduced churn and a greater propensity for them to repurchase, raising your organisation's share of their wallet. While there is an intuitive connection between improved security, increased satisfaction and increased revenue, it is again hard for many organisations to quantify.

In my experience, security and revenue benefits tend to sit outside the call-centre budget, so they are more challenging cases to make, which may leave efficiency as the sole financial benefit. To determine efficiency benefits, the key input is the same data we used in developing the Security Path Visualisation in Chapter 7. You can use this data to estimate the changes in flows between the existing and the new paths that your modern security process will create.

When estimating how these flows will change and the likely efficiency benefits from the changes, you need to make certain assumptions:

- **Coverage** – modern identification methods depend on the quality of your internal data (phone numbers, etc) and the provision of the corresponding data points from the phone network or customer. An offline assessment of this can usually be made using existing data to assess how comprehensive coverage is likely to be.

- **Take-up rate** – some modern authentication methods require the customer's consent, which is obtained through the registration process we will cover in Chapter 12. Although you want to maximise this rate, it is inevitable that a small proportion of customers will decline and not be able to use these methods. For planning purposes, expect take up to be in the 80–90% range.

- **Authentication rate** – all modern authentication methods have a rate of FR. In addition to this, there will be a proportion of callers who are currently authenticated but are not who they claim to be. These may be unsuccessful with modern methods in the future. For planning purposes, expect the authentication rate to be in the 90–98% range.

Detailed calculations are beyond the scope of this book, but you can access a simple benefit calculator tool at www.symnexconsulting.com/unlock-book, which may be helpful in estimating benefits and seeing the impact of different assumptions.

Business case – costs

Every organisation will have its own methods for documenting the costs and benefits of specific proposals, which I will not attempt to detail here. In general, any solution entails implementation and running costs.

The implementation and operating costs will include:

- **Supplier costs** – during implementation, these cover setup, customisation, integration and licensing (if purchased as a perpetual licence). When the solution is operational, supplier costs will include each call or transaction (ie if not purchased as a perpetual licence), ongoing support, performance optimisation and improvements. We will cover engaging with suppliers in Chapter 11.

- **Development costs** – during implementation, these are you or your partners' costs for the changes required to your call-centre platform, customer relationship management (CRM) and line-of-business applications. When the solution is operational, costs include any letters, text messages or other notifications that may be required, as well as an allowance for improvements.

- **Business costs** – during implementation, these cover the time and effort required to manage the project, train customers and create marketing material. They also cover the often-overlooked additional handle time that may be required to enrol customers in modern methods. When the solution is operational, costs include the time and effort required to manage, optimise and improve the solution.

As a rule of thumb, I generally expect the costs in each of these areas to be roughly equal during implementation, unless the integration environment is particularly complex or the scale significant.

While this is all standard from a business-case perspective, there are some unique aspects of a case for modern security methods:

- **Optimisation costs** – as modern methods are probabilistic and based on machine learning, the effectiveness of their decision making has the potential to increase as more data becomes available. Conversely, it can also reduce because of changes to the operating environment, such as introducing new customer groups or increasing the use of different calling devices. Regular assessment of performance is essential, which may require support from specialist suppliers or internal resources.

- **Management** – as modern methods are passive, it's challenging for agents to identify and resolve any issues that customers might have. While these issues are likely to occur far less frequently, there is value in dedicating time and effort to reviewing outcomes both individually and in aggregate to ensure that the service is performing as expected. When customers do experience issues, you are likely to need specialist internal resources to investigate and resolve them.

- **Complexity** – modern methods require near real-time communications and decision making between a variety of different components. In my experience, internal development costs are often underestimated, usually because there is no previous experience of real-time integration between agent desktop and/or CRM, supplier application and call-centre platform. The knock-on effect is to increase cost, extend the duration of the project's implementation costs and delay benefits. The best way to overcome this is to detail broadly the desired customer journeys early on so that all participants understand the work required of them.

Building the emotional narrative

Your emotional case needs to ensure that all stake-holders build a connection with the problem and the opportunities. To be successful, it generally covers three areas.

What does the security process feel like now?

While the numbers from your Security Path Visualisation speak for themselves, they can create detachment from what real customers and agents are facing daily. Wherever possible, encourage stakeholders to complete some form of call-listening or side-by-side observation so that they can get a more vivid picture of the usability and efficiency challenges of the existing process. In a similar way, it can be helpful to review fraud or security incidents to find illustrative examples of how weak the security of the existing process is.

The power of the factlet

While the Security Path Visualisation provides a large amount of information in an easily digestible form, it is often one or two key facts that have the most enduring value. Executives and senior managers just can't help relaying these novel facts to each other, and each retelling strengthens the case for change. In my experience, these facts have made it to the top of the organisation and senior executives have started telling me about the issues with the current process and the implications of them before my recommendations are even complete.

A factlet is widely defined as a standalone and possibly arcane – but nonetheless interesting – statistic or fact. It should not be confused with a factoid, which is completely spurious and made up. Finding the one or two factlets that work for you will depend on how novel (not something anyone has measured or reported before) and unexpected (different to what people would commonly expect) they are for your organisation. My top five recommendations are:

- Percentage of (or average) talk time spent on security
- Number or percentage of callers per year who are denied service having failed security
- Percentage of callers who complete security before speaking to an agent
- Number (or cost) of complaints per year about your security processes
- Number (or cost) of letters, emails, calls related to establishing or resetting passwords and PINs

Do not underestimate the value of these little nuggets or keep them to yourself, as they can be a powerful tool to help change an organisation's perspective on an issue.

What could it be like in the future?

Having ensured everyone understands the current position, you help them build up a picture of what is possible with their support. Many stakeholders will not be able to engage in the detailed calculations and assumptions you make in your benefit case, so you need to find other ways of making this possible future real for them.

The least effective option is likely to be the vendor demonstration. This is great at showing how the technology works, but too sterile or generic to create a connection with the way things could be in the future. The most effective, in my experience, is a mock-up of the optimal future experience. Create an audio recording in which agents role-play themselves and the customer in the future experience and play it back alongside a simple PowerPoint explanation or presentation of potential screens. Stakeholders are far more likely to connect this with their call-listening and side-by-side experiences.

What could happen if we do nothing?

The final part of the case is to illustrate the emotional cost of doing nothing. Some stakeholders may assume that while doing nothing won't improve the situation, at least it won't make it worse, but this is unlikely to be true as the sophistication of fraudsters, the requirements of regulators and the expectations of customers are all increasing. Even with a positive ROI (the business case), clear and present pain (what it's like now) and the promise of a better future (what it could be like), it's difficult to build momentum for change without a burning platform. Again, the exact source of this challenge is likely to vary by organisation, but it will be related to one of usability, efficiency or security.

As brand and reputational risk are not well articulated by the traditional business case, explore these areas to understand if there are any opportunities to illustrate the impact of doing nothing. Some aspects you might consider are:

- **Competitor first-mover advantage** – a competitor could make similar changes before your organisation, receiving industry awards and recognition as a result, which is likely to increase complaints from your customers. Illustrating this could be as simple as showing a mocked-up award, newspaper headline or complaints forecast.

- **Security incident** – it's often only a matter of luck that a major security incident, along with the associated press coverage, has not occurred with your existing processes. Again, illustrate what could happen with a mocked-up press release or newspaper headline.

- **Regulatory changes or investigation** – regulators and governments are increasingly interested in protecting the rights and privacy of consumers. This could lead to legal changes that force improvements or introduce fines for organisations that fail to protect their customers' data. Once again, mocked-up newspaper headlines or press releases can highlight the desirability of making improvements sooner rather than later.

CASE STUDY: TIPPING POINT

Often the case for change is well understood and accepted, both on a rational and emotional level, but it doesn't make the threshold for investment until a tipping point is reached. Here are a few cases of tipping points that I have experienced:

- A utility with big plans to grow a part of its business was struggling to provide a tangible way for its customers to feel improvements and innovation. Call-centre managers made the case that improved security processes could provide this, as well as improve overall efficiency.

- Call-centre managers in another organisation, renowned for being the most customer centric in its industry, used a competitor's announcement of improvements in their security processes to tip the scale in favour of investment.

- A financial services organisation expected that call volume and customer dissatisfaction would increase because of new regulations, so used the opportunity to tie improvements in its security processes to the regulatory change to mitigate the worst effects.

Call listening and executive perception

As call-centre leaders, we spend a significant proportion of our days listening to customers' issues in their own words and voices, so we sometimes forget that others in the organisation don't have the same visceral experience. Many senior executives and subject-matter experts simply don't encounter the organisation's services in the same way that an average customer does.

By virtue of being an employee, a stakeholder is better able to navigate your organisation's security processes than the average customer. While a full-blown customer empathy programme is beyond the scope of this book, I have always found that when stakeholders are directly confronted with some of the challenges of traditional security, it impacts their commitment to supporting change far more than the rational case.

One method of achieving this is to allow stakeholders to sit beside your agents, listening into the call, seeing the same computer screen and chatting with the agent (however briefly) between calls. This way, they see both sides of the problem, expelling any suspicion they may have that you've manipulated the experience to highlight the worst-case scenario.

The risk with this approach is that, because of the limited time available, stakeholders may not experience the worst of your existing processes. Alternatively, their attention may be drawn to the agent's compliance and skills rather than the processes and tools the agent is forced to use.

My preferred method is to use call recordings to identify exemplars of the pain and stress caused by the existing process. These recordings can be used in presentations and discussions, along with a rich picture of the customer's context, to highlight the key pain points.

CASE STUDY: PASSIONATE FEEDBACK

When I worked with a senior call-centre manager at a large bank, I found she was taken aback when an agent focus group on identification and verification processes became particularly animated. They really cared about their customers and the experience they received. While they regularly gave their managers unsolicited feedback on pricing, process and product decisions, they had never done so with such passion as they were now demonstrating for the security process.

In discussing this with the agents later, I realised that everyone just assumed the current process was 'the way that things are done round here' and there was no hope of changing that. They said that denying someone access to the requested service was one of the worst parts of their job, made even more frustrating by the fact that they knew the process wasn't really that secure as there had been a number of successful frauds.

Giving the agents permission to speak at that one session identified half a dozen idiosyncrasies with the existing process that were relatively easy to resolve. More importantly, it provided the manager with the resolve and anecdotal evidence to make her case to the other stakeholders who needed to be influenced to approve change. She'd had no idea her teams cared so much about this issue until she asked.

Reducing uncertainty and delivery risk

When you're planning the implementation of modern security processes, there are likely to be areas of uncertainty that make it challenging to determine the full costs and benefits of any changes. In some cases, these areas are so significant that they risk undermining the viability of the whole project, so you need to address them before progressing.

Areas of uncertainty are likely to fall into these categories:

- **Efficacy** – while the underlying technology is well proven and you can use benchmark values, they may not be appropriate if your particular use case or context is significantly different from the reference cases. To reduce the risk of under- or overestimating benefits, you can use the same technology to conduct offline evaluations or experiments using real-world data, but without the cost or time required for full implementation. These are known as proofs of value.

- **Integration complexity** – in some complex environments, there is a risk that integration will not be feasible or will be significantly more difficult than expected. If external reference cases do not provide sufficient confidence, consider a proof of concept. This is an experimental project that will indicate whether the proposed changes are feasible or not. Establish it as a standalone project without expectation of full implementation to test different approaches.

- **Customer acceptance/adoption** – technologies may have been well received in many industries and use cases, but there may be unique aspects to your customers to consider specifically. You can increase confidence in your choice by using focus groups, but this is unlikely to provide statistically valid estimates for your whole customer population. The best course of action is to conduct a pilot implementation. This will still incur many of the costs of a full implementation, but it should be possible to limit the scope in a way that validates the key assumptions before you commit.

While these are effective methods of mitigating risk, I do not expect many organisations to need to use them as they add their own costs and delay improvements to the security process. In most cases, benchmark assumptions, solution design and external references will be sufficient to provide reassurance.

Summary

Once you've planned your new security process, you will need to persuade stakeholders across your organisation to provide you with the time, resources and support to implement it. In this chapter, we have examined how to make the case in a way that supports these stakeholders' rational and emotional decision making.

The key points we looked at are:

- A large part of the challenge of introducing modern security is convincing stakeholders of the benefit of doing so.

- Making a comprehensive and accurate assessment of the implementation and running costs of your proposed modern security process is vital.

- Benefits include revenue and cost impacts that usually fall outside the call-centre budget and less tangible benefits such as customer satisfaction.

- Encourage senior executives to witness for themselves the frustration for both customers and agents arising from the current security processes.

- Paint a vivid picture of the risks of inaction and the rewards of introducing modern security. This will help to build the case for change.

- Pilots and proofs of concept and value may reduce uncertainty and mitigate some implementation risks, but will increase the costs and duration of the project. Only consider them if they're essential in your organisation's context.

PART THREE

IMPLEMENTING MODERN SECURITY

Implementation of any new technology is a balancing act between the competing pressures of speed and quality, but that doesn't mean you should be afraid to try and achieve both. This section is about the best practice for designing, implementing and optimising modern security methods using the Crawl, Walk, Run framework to ensure you can make safe progress while learning and improving with real customer feedback.

11

A Balancing Act

The detailed design and implementation of modern security requires a delicate balancing act between competing factors. In this chapter, I will show you how to get that balance right by ensuring your modern security methods are adopted by customers while respecting their right to choose, registering the real customer and confirming that the technology is working as you expect.

The value chain

The value chain illustrates the importance of adoption and provides a framework for designing, implementing and optimising modern security methods. There are several steps required before the usability, efficiency and security value of a modern process is realised. It may involve more than one customer call or interaction before the one that creates the value, and during each call there are multiple steps that must be successfully completed.

In simple terms, if the customer is not registered to use the authentication method, then they will be unable to authenticate with it. This goes for both the voiceprints required for voice biometrics and the telephone number required by network authentication. While you may already have a significant amount of phone numbers registered at the outset, the use of the phone number as an authentication method requires that any changes are securely registered. Similarly, you need to be sure to some degree that the caller is who they claim to be before registering their voice for subsequent use with voice biometrics.

It is not until a subsequent call has taken place that the customer will be able to use the new authentication method, and then only if you are able to correctly identify the customer against your records before attempting authentication. Depending on the required performance of the authentication process, a varying proportion of callers will be unable to authenticate despite being who they claim to be.

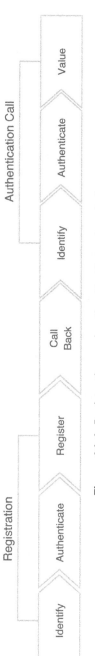

Figure 11.1: *Registration and authentication value chain*

Unfortunately, as with every conversion process, there will be a drop off between each step of the value chain as a certain proportion of customers don't make the transition to the next one. The objective of the design process and ongoing optimisation is to maximise customer adoption and minimise this drop off. As the reasons for the drop off between each step vary significantly, being able to measure the performance of each step is key to enabling subsequent optimisation.

Design for adoption

The technology for modern security methods has existed for some time, but only recently have viable and desirable patterns of implementation been developed and tested. In the context of a security process and modern authentication methods, 'viable' includes regulatory and legal compliance as well as reduction of vulnerabilities.

These patterns were developed using design thinking approaches and provide the basis for my recommendations, but as every organisational context is different, they should be adapted to suit based on the principle of 'design for adoption'. This means making every decision from the perspective of how it will impact customers' acceptance and take up.

My four-step approach for designing modern security methods for adoption is:

1. **Customer** – start with the customer, creating a baseline process that represents what is ultimately most desirable for them. How would the ideal process sound and feel to the customer?

2. **Technology** – consider the constraints of the technology to understand areas of contention and opportunity. Can the technology be adapted, modified or used in a different way to minimise the impact on adoption? Does the technology require any additional processes or process steps (such as enrolment) to be viable?

3. **Regulation** – some methods such as voice biometrics will come with legal obligations that may constrain or influence the design of your process. What additional process steps are needed to meet legal and regulatory obligations? How can you minimise the impact on adoption while meeting these obligations?

4. **Vulnerability** – every process and method will have vulnerabilities. Even if they are almost impossible to exploit, you need to understand them and mitigate them either in the process design or by other means. For this reason, even though technologies like voice biometrics require enrolment before authentication, it is best practice to start with designing the authentication process before moving on to designing a registration process.

Design thinking

The term 'design thinking' was first coined by Tim Brown[18] and the design firm IDEO, and later popularised by them and the Design School at Stanford University. This human-centred approach starts with what is desirable for the customer, then figures out which of these many things are both viable from an economic perspective and feasible from a technical perspective. It's all about finding the sweet spot where these intersect, as in Figure 11.2.

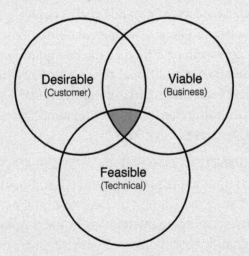

Figure 11.2: Design thinking Venn diagram[19]

18 Brown, T, 'Design thinking' (*Harvard Business Review*, June 2008) https://hbr.org/2008/06/design-thinking, accessed November 2021

19 Adapted from 'Design Thinking Defined' by IDEO, https://designthinking.ideo.com

Design thinking, or derivatives of it, is used by many of the world's most innovative organisations to develop new products and services, as well as to improve existing ones. Its philosophy is at the heart of my approach to designing the security processes that can unlock your call centre.

This approach initially encourages divergent thinking, inspired by a deep understanding of the customer and their pain, to generate a wide range of options. These options are then subject to further ideation and exploration with real customers selecting which to take forward. When options are taken forward, they won't be perfect right away, so simulation and prototypes refine designs, again with input from real customers, before implementation. Even in implementation, the solution won't be perfect straight away, so plan for iteration from the start.

Respecting the customer's right to choose

Many jurisdictions require the customer's consent before their information can be used for biometric identification or authentication. Even when consent isn't required, customers will have different attitudes and perceptions of modern security methods that will affect their acceptance of them.

Biometric authentication methods where there is no active participation from the customer have always suffered from an 'uncanny valley' issue, ie their use makes people uneasy. While it is entirely feasible to create a voiceprint and authenticate a customer without them ever knowing, if this modifies the security process so that they don't now need to go through any authenticating steps, then this absence will create unease and reduce their confidence.

From my earliest experiences with voice biometrics, it's been clear to me that to meet usability and efficiency objectives, its use needs to be overt, which entails engaging the customer during setup. For this reason, I always include an offer of registration in advance of enrolment, even if consent is not required. This ensures that the customer understands the features and benefits of the technology and has a chance to ask questions or express an objection to its use. I also recommend being transparent as to the method used during authentication, to provide reassurance and reinforcement of the positive impact of the technology to the customer.

Regulators have recognised the potential for biometric technology to be misused and the need to protect individuals from those who might do so. In practice, the opportunity for misuse in the call centre is exceptionally limited, but an increasing number of jurisdictions have enhanced existing privacy regulations or introduced new ones. These mostly require a customer's informed consent before any biometric information can be processed.

While the regulations vary and will continue to evolve, this requirement is entirely consistent with the approach I recommend, but it may introduce specific requirements that deviate from what the customer might otherwise have considered desirable. In most cases, these requirements are met by the customer's agreement to specifically worded disclaimers that can be presented after they have been offered the service, but always confirm this with your own legal advisers.

CASE STUDY: GOLD STANDARD SERVICE

Welcome to the hushed and discreet world of the private banker. This well-paid individual is responsible for managing her clients' long-term financial interests, but the problem is that their relationship with her is so close that they want her to be their single point of contact for all their financial transactions, however mundane: standing orders, transfer limits; you name it. Dealing with these routine matters severely limits the time she has available to do what she is paid to do.

My task was to build for these demanding clients a call-centre service that would handle their routine transactions better (and more economically, of course) than a private banker. The real challenge was replicating the experience of speaking to a private banker, not least because private bankers know their clients by their voices.

By taking 'Customers want to be recognised by their voice alone as they talk to an agent' as the starting point and envisaging the future process before making allowances for the available technology, the organisation was able to maintain a vision throughout the development process. At the time, the only implementations of voice-biometric technology relied on a customer speaking a passphrase such as 'My voice is my password' to an automated system, which was clearly inconsistent with the desired experience. Ultimately, technology vendors adapted their solutions to fit the desired process, and even surprised themselves with the results.

Derivatives of the process this organisation created are now used by hundreds of organisations and millions of customers.

Being confident in performance

Your existing security processes may be far from perfect, but their weaknesses and costs are familiar to all from experience. Many stakeholders will outwardly signal their understanding of the modern security approach but will internally be fearful of disrupting the status quo. They need confidence that the solution will perform as expected and are unlikely to be fully convinced by external references.

This is further complicated by the challenge of choosing an appropriate operating threshold. While the general performance characteristics of any technology can be shown using laboratory experiments, these are unlikely to help an organisation decide where the appropriate threshold for its unique combination of technology, customers and risks will lie. This creates a chicken-and-egg problem in which stakeholders are unlikely to agree implementation without evidence and evidence can't be gained without some implementation. Any implementation plan must acknowledge this and seek to build confidence over time while minimising risk.

> 'If you can't fly then run, if you can't run then walk, if you can't walk then crawl, but whatever you do, you have to keep moving forward.'
> — Martin Luther King, Jr[20]

To build confidence in the technology and obtain the data necessary to select appropriate operating thresholds, I recommend a progressive and iterative approach familiar to many, entitled 'Crawl, Walk, Run'. It's loosely based on the famous Martin Luther King Jr quote and similar to those adopted in agile development and innovation organisations. A further advantage of this approach is that it allows you to build confidence not just in security aspects, but also in the usability and efficiency of the design, so developers can learn as they go along and make changes quickly.

The approach comprises the following phases:

---

20 From a speech at Spelman College in April 1960, accessed via YouTube: Olaitan Oyebola, 'If you can't run then walk – Martin Luther' [video] (17 March 2017), www.youtube.com/watch?v=MFOFs0iAwDg, accessed November 2021

- **Crawl** – during the Crawl phase, the solution is only available to a designated and controlled group of customers. Usually, these are employees who are also customers or a specific group of early adopters. This is known as the 'friends and family' phase; while it is biased in its customer selection, it can start to build confidence in processes and performance.

- **Walk** – during the Walk phase, the solution will be made available to a small number of customers who are representative of the wider population. These customers are far more likely to behave in similar ways to the rest of the customer base and the data they provide will give a better indication as to how the full-scale implementation will perform.

- **Run** – the run phase progressively opens the solution to all in-scope customers, monitoring performance for any exceptions to the behaviour and results seen in the previous phases.

Ensure understanding

Moving from traditional and transitional security methods to modern ones has significant benefits for every organisation, but it demands a different way of thinking about the security process. Add to this the potential for misunderstanding about how the technology behind modern methods works, based on media and supplier exposure, and you have an ideal opportunity for confusion and miscommunication. No solution is perfect, no matter how much some reports would have you believe it is.

In all the most successful implementations, a key common factor has been the conscious effort the organisation has made to ensure that all stakeholders understand the concept of modern security, as well as the limitations of the technology. When this doesn't happen, people make decisions and form opinions based on faulty or conflicting mental models. You can watch a short video explainer, which I use to address this issue, at www.symnexconsulting.com/unlock-book.

The process of education allows stakeholders to ask questions that they might consider to be foolish, but which are often pertinent. This education needs to continue throughout the design and implementation process, ideally based on concepts that stakeholders are likely to be familiar with. Nearly everyone seems to understand fingerprinting thanks to exposure to crime dramas, so I often give the process of using fingerprints to find a murder suspect as an example to explain how other forms of biometrics work, including the differences between authentication and identification, as well as the impact of probabilistic versus deterministic decision making.

Engaging with potential suppliers

Supplier selection can be challenging, with every organisation having its own process in a rapidly evolving product and provider landscape. In general, I group the suppliers you'll need to consider into one of three categories:

- **Technology providers** – these companies are experts in the underlying technologies and provide discrete software solutions for a particular area such as voice biometrics or network authentication.

- **Platform providers** – these companies have developed platforms that tie together different technologies and orchestrate their use across the security process. Some may also have their own discrete technologies that can be provided without the platform but will enable integration with others.

- **Solution providers** – these companies have integrated one or more technologies within the context of a wider solution, such as an IVR or contact centre as a service platform. They may have their own discrete technology solutions but are more likely to integrate those of others.

Engaging with the wrong type of supplier for your organisation is likely to misrepresent the cost case.

The right type of supplier for your organisation will reflect the relative risk of your products and services, and the degree of sophistication of your technical capabilities. These capabilities include the capacity for you and your supplier to design, develop, test and implement bespoke solutions.

In some higher-risk organisations, it may be appropriate to procure a discrete technology solution and integrate it with your own applications; in others, it may be more appropriate to procure a platform solution. In lower-risk organisations, solutions integrated with your existing technologies are likely to be the most cost effective and easiest to use.

Figure 11.3: Technology supplier decision matrix

Having determined the right type of supplier for your organisation, you can identify a shortlist for more detailed conversations. The suppliers' directory at www.symnexconsulting.com/unlock-book is a great place to start this search.

Selecting suppliers

There are many factors that will influence the decision on the right supplier for your organisation. In respect to successfully implementing a modern security process, I recommend you keep in mind:

- **Delivery experience** – while underlying technologies continue to evolve and there will be no shortage of impressive features and performance data, the solution you choose must work with your organisation's existing systems. Establish early on, usually through references, the degree of experience the supplier has in working with the technology in your industry and with your existing technology stack (call centre and CRM). A lack of specific experience shouldn't immediately discount a supplier – but weigh it carefully.

- **Price transparency** – every supplier will have a different way of pricing the solution. This in my opinion is designed to prevent you from understanding the real costs and their drivers, and is further complicated by different approaches to pricing on-premises perpetual licences compared with services provided remotely.

Establish a clear pricing methodology that ideally represents the total cost of ownership over the reasonable life expectancy of the solution (three to five years), using your expected call volumes over the same period to assess each supplier based on their cost per call.

- **Performance** – it is easy to produce compelling graphs and statistics demonstrating the relative performance of any one solution. In practice, these impressive statistics are produced using test data that is unlikely to be representative of your real environment. Use these comparisons to establish that suppliers are in the same ballpark rather than one being distinctly better than another. In my experience, the performance differences between suppliers are unlikely to be material to your business outcomes once the impact of process design and implementation decisions is accounted for.

Summary

Modern security methods will only deliver their expected impact if customers adopt them. The value chain highlights the importance of registration before a customer can use the new process to authenticate and value can be created.

During implementation of your modern security process, you need to balance the competing demands of securing registration, maximising adoption, under-standing performance and respecting a customer's right to choose.

The key points we covered are:

- My four-step design approach for implementing modern security methods considers the customer, technology, regulation and vulnerability.

- Follow the Crawl, Walk, Run framework to ensure you can build confidence in process and technology performance progressively in a safe environment.

- All your stakeholders must understand how modern security methods work, so education is essential.

- The key considerations when selecting a supplier are delivery experience, price transparency and performance.

12

Designing For Voice Biometrics

O f all modern caller-authentication methods, passive voice biometrics is the most powerful and effective, but getting implementation right depends on a registration process that maximises customer adoption. In this chapter, I will provide best practice for designing the registration and authentication processes that sit above and around the technology.

Voice-biometric registration

Before authenticating a caller with voice biometrics, you need a voiceprint, which is created during enrolment. A technical process, sometimes referred to as training, creates the voiceprint, but there are several steps to complete before this. The entire process is known as registration.

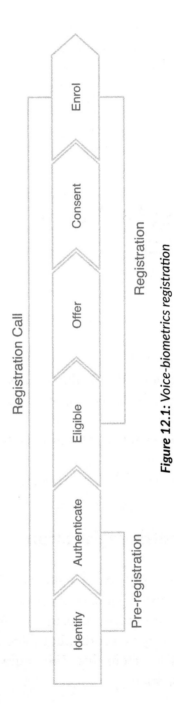

Figure 12.1: *Voice-biometrics registration*

There are specific considerations for voice biometrics:

- **Eligibility** – consider whether there are some customers who you don't want to offer voice biometrics to for security, legal, proposition or technical reasons. If there are current fraud concerns about a customer, for example, make sure you enrol the real customer and not a fraudster. As children's voices change quite significantly around puberty and they may not be legally empowered to give consent, you may wish to exclude them from enrolment. An agent will need to know that the customer is eligible before presenting an offer to them.

- **Offer** – because voice-biometrics authentication is quite different from conventional authentication, you will want to prepare the customer for the changed experience. Even if their consent is not required in your jurisdiction, I would always recommend you allow customers the opportunity to ask questions and object. Also make sure that the same customer is not repeatedly offered the service in a short period of time (if, for example, they call three or four times in a day). It may not be appropriate to offer enrolment on every eligible call.

- **Consent** – this step usually requires the customer's positive agreement to a formal disclosure statement, such as 'Please confirm that you are happy for XYZ Bank to store and process your voice to provide you with secure access to your accounts'. Your legal or compliance department will be able to advise on the correct wording and steps for your situation.

- **Enrolment** – while the majority of audio for enrolment is captured before and during registration, some additional audio may still be required, and there are technical reasons why a voiceprint may fail to be created. Confirm to a caller when their voiceprint has been created so you can manage their expectations for future calls. To mitigate the risk of imposter enrolment and fulfil other legal obligations, many organisations also choose to send text messages, emails or letters confirming that the customer is now registered and providing more information about how to use the service.

Why don't customers accept offers or provide consent?

In speaking to hundreds of customers and listening to thousands of offer and consent conversations, I have discovered that there is a simple set of needs to be met before a customer will agree to using a new security

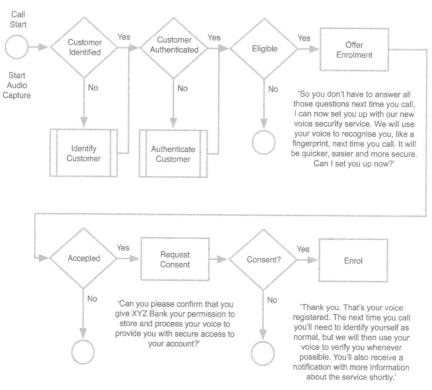

Figure 12.2: *Example voice-biometrics registration process*

process. The absence of any one element will prevent them from doing so:

- **Understanding** – the customer needs at least some understanding of how the new process will work. It doesn't have to be that detailed as many customers already have a basic understanding from their use of similar technologies, such as those on their smartphone or with other organisations. There is a risk that some customers will be confused by over-explanation, so it's better to be succinct but prepared for some customers who will need more detail.

- **Incentive** – it needs to be clear to the customer what they are getting out of the arrangement. While this might seem obvious, it's always helpful to emphasise the improvements a customer can expect in the future. You can make a case based on whatever is most important to them, whether it be speed, ease of use or security, compared with existing methods.

- **Trust** – the customer needs to trust you to use a new security process in a positive way. Many organisations already have this trust, but you need to be prepared to explain the safeguards around its use and the customer's rights over the data if necessary.

- **Usability** – the registration process must be usable. The more steps it takes to complete, the less likely the customer is to do so. To the extent allowed by legislation, keep the number of steps and their complexity to an absolute minimum.

Different personality types process the information they receive and make decisions differently. For the purpose of registration, I generally divide these into active and reflective, although the division is not entirely binary.

In my experience, most callers are already in an active mode when they're calling. Provided the four needs are met, they are likely to give a positive response to the offer of voice biometrics as an authentication method, but a significant minority of callers will be unwilling to decide during the call, even with these needs met. These callers need time to reflect on it and often respond to the offer with statements such as 'I don't have time today' or 'I'm happy with the existing process, thank you'.

While skilful agents can handle these objections and may convert a proportion of reflective customers to a positive response, it is often not worth prolonged conversations or multiple attempts. It is far better to annotate their record to the effect that a first offer has been made, so that offers on subsequent calls can reflect this fact. You may consider using other channels, such as email or messaging reminders with information to support the customer's reflections, so that the next time they are asked, they have had an opportunity to decide.

You can find some more specific recommendations on how to offer enrolment in Chapter 14.

Reactive vs proactive registration

In most cases, registration is completed during a call initiated by the customer to fulfil another intent:

this is the reactive approach. In my experience, this is the least expensive way to implement new technology; while there is a small increase in handle time to complete the offer and consent process, there is no overall increase in call demand. The impact of this handle time on the call-centre operation can be managed by either limiting the number of agents able to offer registration or ensuring the offer and eligibility rules keep the impact within available capacity.

The disadvantage with the reactive approach is that it does depend on customers calling, and as some don't call very often, it can take a long time to register a significant proportion of the customer base. Those customers who don't call frequently are in fact those most likely to benefit, as they are the ones who tend to experience challenges with the existing security processes.

You could consider a proactive approach to bring forward customer registrations, but evaluate it carefully to ensure it creates sufficient value to be worthwhile. The most common method is to use an existing welcome or onboarding process. These calls are generally initiated by the organisation and registration can be added to the process with minimal cost, although it will need to be prioritised against all the demands on time for other business objectives. Where there are periodic account reviews or any other outbound calls initiated by the organisation, registration can be added to these processes, as long as you ensure that answering machines and receptionists are not accidentally enrolled.

Securing voice-biometric registration

It may be counterintuitive, but I recommend you allow customers to register regardless of the authentication method they use on the registration. The greater the confidence you have in their initial authentication during registration, the better, but don't prevent customers from enrolling just because they have not used a certain authentication method.

With knowledge- and possession-based authentication, you cannot be certain that the caller presenting in two different sessions is the same person. Just because the first caller is successful doesn't necessarily mean that the next caller will be the same person. The knowledge-based credentials could have been overheard, stolen or even guessed, allowing an imposter to authenticate on subsequent sessions. Similarly, there is a possibility, albeit lower, that a possession-based device may have been lost or compromised between the two calls.

This is exactly the point of inherence-based authentication. With this type of authentication, you can be certain that, provided there is a successful match, the caller on each subsequent call is the same person who enrolled.

The graph in Figure 12.3 demonstrates this effect.

The graph shows an arbitrary but constant-over-time level of confidence in two different authentication methods. Assuming that a caller is enrolled for voice-biometrics authentication following an initial call using knowledge-based authentication, the confidence starts at the same level, but increases over time as the caller interacts with the call centre. Because we can be almost certain that subsequent calls are from the same person who enrolled and if no transactions have been repudiated or customer reports received, it can theoretically become more secure than the possession-based method over time. Ultimately, it becomes constant and flattens out at the same level as the FA threshold of the system.

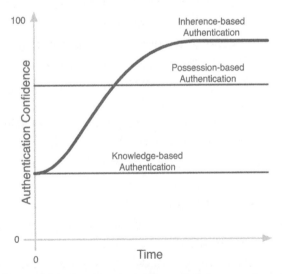

Figure 12.3: *Increased confidence in inherence-based authentication over time*

Most enrolments will be from genuine customers. Even if an imposter does enrol, then at least no other imposters will be able to authenticate using voice biometrics. Given that they could already authenticate sufficiently to enrol, there is no net increase in risk to the organisation.

The result is that all enrolments reduce the available attack surface for fraudsters. As the proportion of customers who are enrolled increases, the fraudster success rate will naturally decline, as illustrated in Figure 12.4.

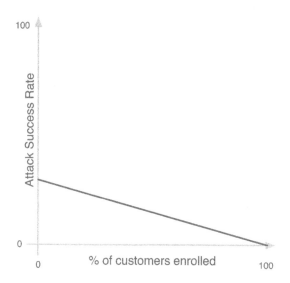

Figure 12.4: Coverage as enrolment increases

Starting with a theoretical 20% fraudster success rate from legacy (knowledge- or possession-based) authentication methods, you can see that as the proportion of customers enrolled for inherence-based authentication increases, the average attack success rate falls. Fraud is squeezed into a smaller group of calls.

CASE STUDY: CUSTOMER FOCUS GROUPS AND SIMULATIONS

To build confidence in inherence-based security designs, I often use customer focus groups with simulations of the proposed process. Here are some of the most memorable moments from these groups:

- When a bank employee asked whether the customer trusted the bank to use their voice for authentication, they replied, 'I trust you with my money, why wouldn't I trust you with my voice?'

- When asked to explain how voice biometrics works, one early adopter customer said, 'Your voice is like a fingerprint.' I have found this to be a far more successful explanation than anything I could come up with.

- Another financial services organisation testing different brand names for a service got the response, 'Why don't you just call it what it is?'

I would encourage you to test and prototype your process design with real customers as early and often as possible. You can rely on them to be straight with you.

Authentication

When an enrolled customer calls back, they can authenticate with their voiceprint. Before they can do this, the system will need to know which voiceprint to check against, so an identification step is required. In a modern security process, this step should be done passively, ideally before the call even connects to the agent. But this isn't always possible.

Figure 12.5: Voice-biometrics authentication

Only a few seconds of customer audio is needed for authentication. Sometimes even the short utterances provided in a speech-driven IVR system or in response to a NLU prompt may be enough. If insufficient audio is provided in an automated system, then the caller can be prompted to clarify their request or identity so you can get more audio.

There are two outcomes from the authentication process: either the caller scores above the threshold or they don't. I refer to this as a match or a mismatch respectively. Of course, it is possible to use the score produced as a direct measure of confidence (or lack thereof), but the resulting variation in treatment is difficult both to explain to customers and to operationalise for agents. The score does, however, have some use in fraud detection and analytics.

Given that, even in industries with high rates of fraudster attack, most callers who get a mismatch result are genuine customers, you need a mismatch process that treats the customer respectfully and allows alternative authentication where feasible. To mitigate the risk of a fraudster deliberately failing inherence-based authentication to exploit weaknesses in legacy authentication, the mismatch outcome still needs to form part of a risk-based decision framework for the range of services and transactions available to the caller. Remember that even if the caller isn't the genuine customer, their intent may not be malicious, such as the case of a daughter supporting her elderly and vulnerable father to navigate a complex process or problem.

Fraud detection

If you're using voice biometrics for authentication, then over time, most callers will be enrolled and you can be confident that they are who they claim to be. There is still some risk that calls will come from enrolled imposters or as the result of an FA, but the calibration process (see Chapter 14) will ensure that this is within your risk appetite (ie the level of risk your organisation is prepared to tolerate before taking action to reduce it).

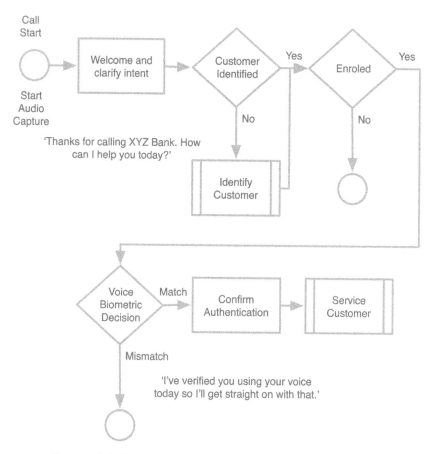

Figure 12.6: *Example voice-biometrics authentication process*

What's in a name?

Human behaviour is heavily influenced by the language we use and its association with our previous experiences. The word 'fail' can be associated with negative experiences, from failed school exams through to systems failures in the workplace.

In a call centre, 'fail' is most likely to be used to describe a caller who has been unable to complete the security process successfully, so must be treated with suspicion and probably denied service. Its use abdicates responsibility from the agent, process and organisation on to the caller, providing the agent with an excuse to assume the caller isn't who they claim to be and allowing them to adopt the persona of defender, even though nearly all 'failures' are genuine customers.

With traditional security methods, the customer will probably accept this responsibility – they assume it's their fault they couldn't remember something or manage the mental gymnastics of giving the correct digits. Only on reflection might they consider that the organisation failed to design an appropriate process or provide alternatives. With modern methods that are probabilistic and don't require callers to do anything, if a genuine caller receives a negative outcome, they are largely blameless.

I recommend you use the words 'mismatch' and 'match' as opposed to 'fail' and 'pass' when talking about the outcomes of modern security methods. If you and your colleagues adopt this language early on in the design and implementation process and use it consistently, it permeates everyone's thinking. This creates more customer-centric processes and, ultimately, outcomes, even for those callers who don't match.

While the voice-biometrics system has not been able to authenticate callers when they mismatch or are not registered (Figure 12.7), it will have captured sufficient audio to use for detection purposes. This captured audio can be compared against watch lists of known fraudsters who have been enrolled by fraud analysts into the system. The targets on these watch lists are usually identified during the investigation process that follows a report of fraud. Audio from newly identified fraudulent calls can then be used to create an enrolment that other calls can subsequently be checked against. Even if a fraudster has not previously been identified, the fact that the same speaker is claiming to be many different customers can identify callers worthy of further investigation.

Both voice-biometrics detection capabilities can be deployed in either real-time, where the results are used to influence the process of an ongoing call (such as routing to a specialist agent), or offline, where they are reviewed by fraud analysts to identify accounts and customers at risk. In both cases, specialist resources are required to manage watch lists and the results of other analytics.

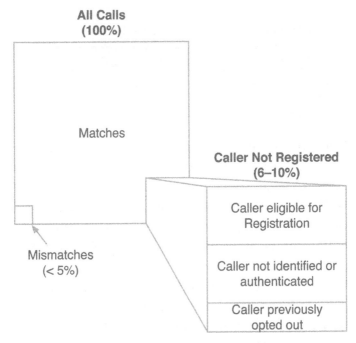

All Calls (100%)

Matches

Mismatches (< 5%)

Caller Not Registered (6–10%)

Caller eligible for Registration

Caller not identified or authenticated

Caller previously opted out

Figure 12.7: Voice-biometrics fraud-detection call types

Detection tasks constitute identification, so in many cases, they bring a far higher risk of false alarm than authentication: because they are required to make many more comparisons, the probability of error is greater. As a result, I recommend that you combine the results of these tasks wherever possible with data from other detection systems and line-of-business applications to create a more holistic assessment of risk and prioritise investigative resources.

Mismatch maths

We can highlight the point that most mismatches are genuine customers mathematically. Even in industries with a high fraudster attack rate, perhaps only 1 in 500 calls comes from a fraudster. If we therefore assume that fewer than 5% of genuine callers are incorrectly rejected (FR), for the reasons we've outlined, but that 99% of imposters are correctly rejected (TR)[21] from 1 million calls, then we can expect 2,000 to be from imposters and the remainder from genuine customers. Unfortunately, almost 50,000 of these customers will be incorrectly rejected (5%). Nearly all the fraudsters will also receive a mismatch result, but of all calls receiving a mismatch, fewer than 4% will be from imposters. If you want to see the calculations for yourself or try out different assumptions, then try the calculator on my website at www.symnexconsulting.com/unlock-book.

Summary

To exploit the potential of voice biometrics to the full, you need as many customers to adopt it as possible. In this chapter, we have looked at designing registration and authentication processes that will help you to ensure they do so.

---

21 I would expect most systems to perform at least this well if not better, but these numbers have been chosen for ease of calculation.

The main topics we covered are:

- The voice-biometrics registration process includes six steps: identify, authenticate, establish eligibility, make an offer, obtain consent and enrol.

- Ensuring that customers understand the advantages of voice biometrics and trust the process will maximise the chances of them accepting an offer to enrol.

- Don't prevent customers from enrolling for voice-biometrics authentication just because they have not used a certain authentication method on the registration call.

- It's important to design a mismatch process for voice-biometrics authentication that doesn't compromise security, but which recognises that most users will be genuine customers.

- Voice biometrics can be used as a fraud-detection tool in calls where the customer hasn't authenticated with it.

13

Designing For Network Data

For many organisations, network data associated with the incoming phone call can support identification, authentication and fraud detection. Even when identification and authentication are not possible, the same data makes it easy to identify the highest-risk calls and apply different treatments to reduce fraud risk.

In this chapter, I will provide the best practice for designing the business processes that exploit network data to the full.

Withheld and unavailable numbers

In most countries, the calling party has a right to withhold their number when calling someone to protect their privacy. Some customers will have this configured as the default behaviour for their line, and some communications providers will present the number as withheld if they have concerns about its origin.

Often, your customers use different network providers to your organisation, and it's not unusual for phone calls to be routed through several providers before reaching your call centre. For billing purposes and to facilitate routing, these networks exchange more information than just the presentation number with each other. Even when there is enough information for routing and billing, some networks don't provide a presentation number at all, so these calls are labelled as unavailable.

It is unrealistic, therefore, to expect that all calls will provide an incoming number. Without an incoming number, you cannot identify or subsequently authenticate the caller using network data, but your communications provider can use the associated data for fraud-detection purposes.

Phone number registration and data quality

Organisations must have a good understanding of the quality of their phone number data before using network data for identification and authentication. Although you might assume that it will be easy to use for identification and authentication purposes, many organisations' customer databases have not been designed to be used in this way, so you first need to address several issues:

- **Number formatting** – there is an agreed international standard (E.164) for phone numbers that will be used by your communications provider (+441234456789, for example) when they're presenting phone numbers. Unfortunately, many organisations do not store numbers in this way. In most cases, the international prefix data is missing or inconsistent, and sometimes, the field may contain text such as spaces and brackets as well as numbers. Some clean-up is inevitably required. Searching on the last eight to nine digits alone works for most organisations.

- **Accuracy** – as phone numbers are likely to have been captured by many different processes and people over time, some will inevitably be incorrect or outdated. When providing a phone number is mandatory in business processes, customers and employees may provide random or nonsense numbers to meet the requirement. Some common 'filler' numbers may need to be excluded from searches, and other constraints on age or source of the phone number may need to be included.

- **Multiple phone numbers per customer** – most organisations allow customers to provide different phone numbers such as home, work and mobile, or daytime and evening. Correctly identifying a customer may entail searching against several fields, all of which may present the above issues.

To estimate the scale of the problem, I recommend an offline analysis of recent call data sourced from the call-centre platform against available organisation data sources. From this process, estimate the likely levels of no number, match, multiple matches and no match responses. Further comparison of this data with known customer contact records will help you to identify other data-quality issues, such as when a number was provided, but no customer record matched.

If the quality of existing data is poor, consider building a new database based on the numbers customers use when calling. Following identification and authentication by other means, agents or automated systems can ask callers to confirm if they wish to register the phone they are calling on today as theirs for subsequent security use. This process may look similar to the voice-biometrics registration process (see Chapter 12) except for the formal consent disclosure requirement.

Any business process that changes customer phone numbers has the potential to create a vulnerability that could be exploited by fraudsters. In addition to a discrete registration process, put appropriate controls in place to ensure that phone numbers are registered correctly.

Identification

When the phone number is provided and you have good records of customer numbers, network data is the easiest way of identifying callers. It requires no customer effort and only the most rudimentary of queries against your records for success. Aim for identification as early as possible in the call, ideally as soon as it connects with your call-centre platform. Understanding the caller's identity, even without authentication, provides valuable information for making better routing and automation decisions.

Often, the incoming number is a mobile number which should match against a single customer record, but your process will need to handle cases where there is more than one match, no match or no number provided. There may be some phone numbers in your records that have dozens if not hundreds of customers associated with them, because of either data-quality issues or a genuine relationship between the customers, for example they have the same employer. Similarly, some numbers come up frequently, such as those related to an employer's switchboard. I would recommend you specifically exclude these high-frequency numbers from number-based identification and authentication to simplify other parts of the process.

When more than one customer matches a number, then you need some form of disambiguation between customers. Ideally, you want to know who the customer is before you route their call, and you want to identify them in an automated way.

The simplest disambiguation identifiers for a customer to recall (in order of ease) are their name, date of birth and address. Of these, date of birth is the easiest to automate and least open to misinterpretation or miskeying by agents, so I recommend using this whenever possible. Customers' postal or zip codes can be used as an alternative, but they are harder to automate. In organisations that don't wish to use an automated system, agents can ask the customer their name and select from a list, provided the list of possible candidates is small (fewer than five or six).

These disambiguation processes represent a reasonably low cognitive load on the caller, but like any challenge, will require some effort to complete. With the latest speech-to-text technology, it is possible to automate many of these requests, but some form of fuzzy logic will be required, based on partial matches, to account for transcription errors.

When using this approach in an automated system, you run the risk that any difference in treatment between recognised and not-recognised numbers can be exploited by fraudsters. By spoofing different numbers and making a call to your IVR system, they can confirm whether a number belongs to a customer, and then use this information to target your customer.

I advise mitigating this risk by using network fraud-detection capabilities to highlight any spoofing before caller identification. If these capabilities highlight a risk, you will clearly need an alternative treatment for the caller that does not confirm the number they've presented belongs to a known customer. Alternatively, you can partially mitigate the risk by asking all callers a disambiguation question such as date of birth and only indicating that the caller has been recognised after authentication.

For callers whose number doesn't match the one on your records or who don't provide one, you'll need a fallback process. It is sometimes practical to ask for their mobile number, as this is easy to automate and for the customer to recall, but evaluate the customer's experience of this approach carefully. It could create significant dissonance with their reason for calling – unless your organisation is the mobile network provider.

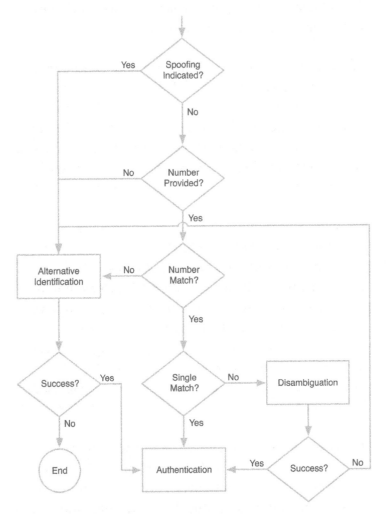

Figure 13.1: *Example phone number identification decision tree*

Authentication

Authentication through a phone number is a possession-based method. It provides confidence that the number presented is genuine and still in the possession of the identified customer.

While identification using network data can, in most cases, be completed via existing call-centre technologies, authentication needs access to additional communications-provider data. This is most often supplied by vendors as a service that analyses and interprets this data. The result is a score that you can use to indicate whether the number presented is the originating number or that the call could be fraudulent in some way.

The data, processes and algorithms used to determine this score are unique to each vendor, but usually cover one or more of these three capabilities:

- **Spoofing detection** – this is analysis of routing data to determine if the call originated from a trusted network and not one that is known to allow spoofing. Depending on their level of network access, some vendors can also determine the current on-hook/off-hook status of the calling party line to determine if it is being used to make a call.

- **Number ownership** – vendors subscribe to data feeds from network providers to identify numbers that have recently been reassigned, mitigating the risk that this has been done fraudulently. As phone numbers are owned by the network provider and not the individual, they can often be reassigned within and between networks.

- **Device ownership** – in addition to the phone number itself, some vendors also provide information about the unique identification number of the mobile device used. This identifier can change between individual calls when, for example, the customer gets a new handset. If it remains the same over a long period, it further increases authentication confidence.

Only when you have high confidence that the number presented is genuine and still in possession of the identified customer can you consider the call authenticated. The three capabilities above mitigate most third-party fraud, but there is still a risk that parties related to the customer can gain access to the genuine device and use it for either legitimate or malicious reasons, so some additional authentication steps may be required to secure higher-risk transactions.

The score is provided nearly instantaneously, so an authentication decision can be made at the start of the call. Then callers that are not considered authenticated can be presented with alternative authentication methods in the IVR system.

Fraud detection

When a caller's number is not available or not recognised, they cannot be authenticated, but the techniques we have already looked at, along with some additional ones, can assess the risk that the call is fraudulent. Vendors use a range of data to make this assessment, but generally the same scoring system to indicate the risk of a call being fraudulent.

The additional techniques include:

- **Regularity** – tracking the frequency of calls from different numbers as it would be unusual for most legitimate callers to call frequently.

- **Association** – tracking the claims of identity made by the caller using each number. In most cases, it would be unusual for a single number to be associated with more than a handful of customers. This is dependent on your systems passing callers' claims of identity on to the vendor application.

- **Watch list** – whether the number presented appears on a list of known or suspected fraudulent callers sourced from your post-event fraud investigations and analysis of historic data. This requires a business process to identify numbers to add and to manage the watch list.

- **Reputation** – like watch lists but sourced from the vendor's other customers (it's sometimes known as a consortium or network watch list) or from analysis of wider network traffic, a reputation can either be positive (associated with known genuine customer behaviour) or negative (associated with suspicious or known fraudulent behaviour).

- **Withheld numbers** – while all the above analysis could be developed internally using data already available to your call-centre platform, it would be easily circumvented by fraudsters withholding their phone numbers. Vendors with network provider relationships can carry out the same analysis of withheld numbers while maintaining compliance with privacy regulations.

- **Acoustics** – some vendors have developed algorithms to identify the audio characteristics that different devices and networks inherently add to the call. They use these to analyse the silent portions of the call to identify anomalies between previous or expected signatures and the current call.

Scoring ranges

The same score is used for authentication and fraud-detection purposes, so the subsequent treatment of a call should be a function of both its identification status and score. Establish three score ranges to help you determine the appropriate treatment strategy:

- **High risk** – calls that are very likely to be fraudulent in some way because they have one or more indicators of attempted fraud. There is still some risk of a false alert even with this group, but it is typically a small percentage of the calls categorised this way. These tend to be referred to as red calls.

- **Some risk** – calls where there are some risk indicators, but there is still a reasonable probability that the caller is genuine, can occur when the customer is roaming on an uncommon overseas network, for example. These are typically referred to as amber calls.

- **Low risk** – calls at the top end of this group are likely to have positive indicators of genuine customer behaviour, such as consistent device usage, but at the lower end, there may simply be the absence of any suspicious indicators. It is unlikely that these calls are fraudulent. They are typically referred to as green calls.

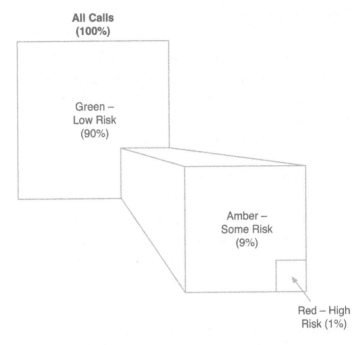

All Calls
(100%)

Green –
Low Risk
(90%)

Amber –
Some Risk
(9%)

Red – High
Risk (1%)

Figure 13.2: *Typical network authentication and fraud-detection score distribution*

Determine the specific threshold scores between these ranges based on an analysis of your live call traffic.

High-risk call treatment

With the benefit of a fraud-detection score or rating, it is possible to vary the treatment of the call to understand further or mitigate the associated risk. In designing these treatments, keep in mind the proportion of calls that are likely to be false alarms and the impact of your chosen treatment strategy on genuine customers.

There is always the option to deny service or automatically terminate the highest-risk calls, but doing so tells the fraudster that their method has been identified and encourages them to try different approaches which may have a lower detection rate. In addition, it denies you the opportunity to understand which accounts or services the fraudster intends to target, and how.

An automated system allowing the highest-risk calls to progress to at least the identification process allows you to understand which customers are compromised and consider additional protection or surveillance to prevent them from being compromised in other channels. Allowing a suspected fraudster to progress to authentication and even provide transaction information may yield valuable insights to prevent future attacks or protect customer assets. Some organisations go as far as to allow the fraudster to think they have been successful on the call, so that they remain unaware of the methods used to detect them.

Human agents can gain similar information but are open to social engineering. There is a greater chance that they may inadvertently tip off the fraudster or be tricked into bypassing controls if they're aware of the call's risk assessment. For this reason, ideally route high-risk calls to specialist fraud agents. Even though this variation in routing and attitude can tip off fraudsters, these agents are typically best placed to identify the few false alarms and understand the fraudster's intent without compromising the means of detection.

As specialist agents are scarce and valuable resources, there is some case for denying service to the most prolific types of attack when there are insufficient resources available. This can result in other fraudster modus operandi being discovered.

Putting it all together

Network-data authentication and fraud detection can be used in several ways, depending on the identification status of the call and number availability.

The performance of this process is a function of several key measures, most of which can be estimated in advance of implementation to assess the size of the opportunity:

- **Inbound number availability** – the proportion of inbound calls that have a valid number presented and available.

- **Number match rate** – the proportion of available inbound numbers that match one or more records in your system.

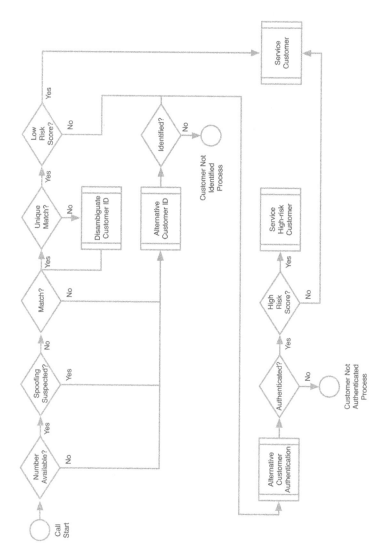

Figure 13.3: Example network-data authentication process

- **Number unique match rate** – the proportion of matched numbers that are subsequently resolved to unique matches through disambiguation or only having one match.

- **Authentication rate** – the proportion of uniquely matched numbers that are scored as low-risk calls so can be considered authenticated.

- **High-risk rate** – the proportion of calls that are scored as high risk so require alternative treatments.

Summary

In this chapter, we looked at designing the business processes that exploit network data to the full. The key points we covered are:

- Network data can be used in several ways depending on the identification status of the call, along with internal data availability and quality.

- Identification matches inbound numbers to your customer records. It is dependent on the availability of the number and quality of your data.

- Authentication follows identification if you have high confidence the number has not been spoofed and is still in the possession of the genuine customer.

- Fraud detection is useful when authentication is not possible. It uses other characteristics of the call to assess the risk that it is fraudulent.

- The three score ranges to help you determine the appropriate treatment strategy for a call are high risk (red), some risk (amber) and low risk (green).

- Make sure you consider the effect your treatment strategy for high-risk calls will have on genuine customers in the case of false alarms.

14

Implementation

To deliver on the promise of modern security, your implementation plan needs to be as robust as the process design. You must ensure that the system operates as expected, you get the right balance of speed and quality during implementation, and frontline colleagues are as well prepared as possible to introduce the new service to customers.

In this chapter, I will provide you with a framework for planning implementation that offers the optimal balance of these competing demands and enables effective decision making.

Incremental implementation

I introduced the Crawl, Walk, Run approach in Chapter 11. This approach allows you to understand the key features in a controlled environment (Crawl) before exposing them to a sample of customers to learn how they react (Walk), and then extending the process to the whole customer base (Run).

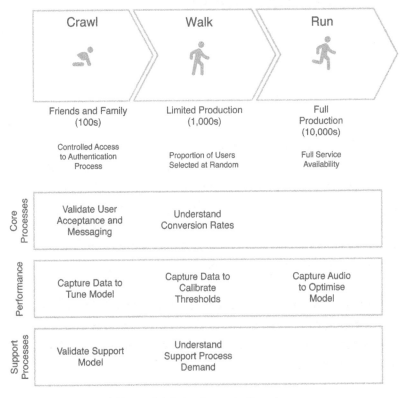

Figure 14.1: Implementation steps

Even though an approach that emphasises the inevitability of changes between phases might seem inefficient, in my experience, it actually accelerates delivery. Stakeholders feel less need to engage in lengthy hypothetical and often circular discussions, which are the biggest source of delays, because they are confident any issues can be resolved later with the benefit of objective data.

There are three key areas where you need to build understanding and confidence within your organisation to be successful:

Core processes

The identification, authentication and registration customer journeys you developed during the design phase will benefit from feedback from customers and agents. The softer elements of these journeys are difficult to test, even with customer focus groups, so their exposure to a wider range of potential customers will inevitably generate valuable insights.

Inviting a representative sample of real customers to experience these journeys is often your first opportunity to validate your value-chain assumptions. Their feedback can prompt a rethink of major design decisions, particularly with voice biometrics, on factors such as eligibility requirements or positioning of customer offers in the call.

Performance

You will know the general performance characteristics of your selected modern authentication methods in advance of implementation, but the profile of your organisation's customers and their call mix will create variation within this range. The best way to establish appropriate thresholds is with the real data gained from the Crawl, Walk, Run approach, which also provides the opportunity to tune the technology to your specific operating environment.

Support processes

The design process focuses on the primary customer journey, but you will need some additional supporting business processes, depending on which modern methods you've chosen. These are often enabled by the vendor and existing business applications and operated by subject-matter experts (who are also needed to support other aspects of implementation).

These processes (detailed in Chapter 15) are difficult to test without real-world data. Even though you can make assumptions about demand levels and mix, they are usually closely correlated to the overall value chain, so it makes little sense to build a substantial capability until you have validated these assumptions.

I would generally expect the Crawl and Walk phases to last anything between two and eight weeks, depending on the complexity of the overall proposition and the amount of data required to tune and calibrate the underlying technology appropriately.

CASE STUDY: WALK WITH YOUR BEST CUSTOMERS

More than one of my clients has chosen to launch into the Walk phase with some of their most valuable customers first. For one investment management company, its most valuable customers were among its most frequently calling. Because of their value, these customers had been allocated to a dedicated group of some of the company's most experienced agents. This made it far easier to control the implementation, identification and investigation of issues as the agents were based in just two different sites with few of their calls overflowing to other groups. More importantly, these agents had the confidence to try different offer approaches and feed back on what was and wasn't working.

For their part, the customers appreciated that their loyalty and value had been recognised by the company inviting them to be the first to try out new approaches. While many of them had no issues with the traditional knowledge-based approach, it became clear that most had just been tolerating it and welcomed the improvement. They were not afraid to express their opinions and provide the company with even more valuable feedback to improve the service. Even though their calling behaviour may not have been fully representative of the wider customer base, because they called more frequently, it was far quicker to gather the data than it would have been with any alternative groups.

While it may appear counterintuitive to burden your most valuable customers with testing new technology, this case study shows there are some significant advantages to asking for their feedback first. It's now a strategy I consider for every client.

Agent training

The biggest difference between organisations that successfully implement new call-centre security processes and those that don't lies in the rate at which agents offer the new service to eligible customers and the proportion of these customers who provide their consent. In my experience, these two factors are heavily influenced by agent advocacy, confidence and skill, all of which can be developed through training and improved over time with coaching and suitable incentives.

Some aspects of agent training can be delivered in classrooms or through e-learning, but the most effective way of learning is through doing. When you're designing your agent training, ensure it includes these aspects:

- **Understanding** – give agents a basic understanding of how the technology works and the opportunity to use it themselves to build advocacy.

- **Explaining** – while some organisations prefer to script the initial offer, I have found it more helpful to provide guidelines and examples rather than be too prescriptive. During training and practical exercises, agents can develop their own way of explaining the service and tailor their language to the nature of the call. Typical guidelines are:

  - What's in it for the customer? Ensure the customer understands the benefits and tailor the offer as appropriate. For example, after a painful traditional authentication experience, the agent could finish their explanation with '…so we don't have to take so long next time.'

  - How does it work? Often, a simple analogy works, such as 'We can use your voice (or phone number) like a fingerprint to confirm your identity.'

  - Less is more. Don't over-explain the service; allow the customer to express any objections early and deal with them before asking a question such as 'Would you like me to set that up now?'

- **Objection handling** – prepare agents to handle typical objections. Again, provide guidelines rather than prescriptive responses to allow agents to tailor their language and sound more natural. Typical objections and guidelines include:

  - 'Not enough time today' – the customer is likely to be reflecting and buying time to decide, so reiterate that there's no effort needed to set the new process up.

  - 'I don't think it's secure' – the customer may not understand how it works, so reiterate and set out how secure it is compared with traditional authentication.

  - 'I'm happy with the existing process' – again, the customer is likely to be buying time to decide, so reiterate relevant benefits or list additional benefits, such as security, that you may not have mentioned in the original offer.

  - 'I'm worried about…' – the customer is likely to have a specific concern that you need to address.

- **Process knowledge** – agents need to know which buttons to press and how to handle exceptions, such as those customers who object on principle and ask not to be approached for consent again, those who change their mind after initially enrolling or those who experience difficulties during authentication.

If agents can practise these exchanges in a safe environment with colleagues, trainers or coaches before speaking to real customers, they are likely to be more confident. If this is not possible, floorwalkers and team leaders can support agents through their first few attempts and help them understand how to improve. Though it is possible to improve agent performance over time, it takes significantly more effort than establishing an effective starting state, so use the Crawl and Walk implementation phases to assess the effectiveness of your training.

Tuning and calibration

In Chapter 1, we used a graph to illustrate the trade-off between security and convenience in all authentication methods. Unlike traditional and transitional methods, which exist in a fixed position in that space, modern authentication methods provide organisations with a choice as to where in that space they wish to operate.

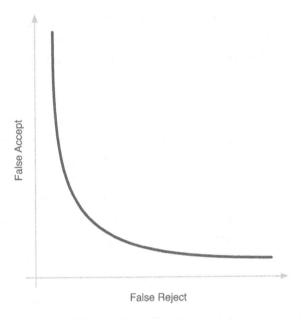

Figure 14.2: *Calibration curve*

The trade-off between FAs (security) and FRs (convenience) can be represented by a curve, allowing organisations to select from a range of operating positions. Calibration is the process that enables us to understand and draw this FA and FR trade-off, as it allows us to look at it in a specific operating environment.

At the same time as enabling calibration, the data gained in the Crawl and Walk phases can be used to tune the underlying algorithms. These algorithms will have been trained in advance using large data sets to understand the features that differentiate most speakers in voice biometrics or identify most fraudulent calls for network authentication, but there is an opportunity to modify the weighting of different features in the overall decision, based on your unique customers.

This process will improve the performance of the system. You can see the extent of this by plotting the calibration curves of the un-tuned and tuned system side by side.

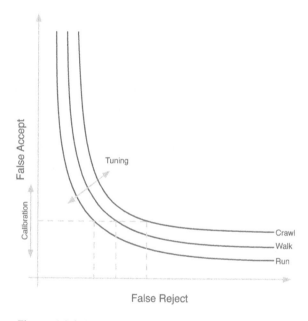

Figure 14.3: *Performance impact of tuning over time*

As tuning progresses with more data from each phase of implementation, the algorithm delivers a lower level of FR at the same level of FA, improving convenience over time.

Tuning and calibration for voice biometrics

In the case of voice biometrics, calibration uses true user imposter testing (TUIT). In these tests, audio obtained from real users simulates an imposter trying to gain access. The curve, like the one in Figure 14.2, can be created by joining the points created when the FR rate and FA rate are calculated and plotted for each available score based on the TUIT sample (ie if the threshold score was 2, then 1% of imposters were accepted and 3% of genuine speakers were rejected).

Even though it's possible to have a high degree of statistical confidence in FA performance based on only a few hundred samples, understanding the FR performance needs many genuine customer authentication attempts. The test assumes that the sample is representative of the eventual customer base, which it may not be if employees and their close contacts are used during the initial phases. Also, the period over which the data is collected will be relatively short, so won't reflect how customers' voices might change over time. Furthermore, a TUIT depends on the audio being attributed to the right customer, so any imposter audio captured in the sample needs to be identified and removed, often manually, after you have listened to it.

During implementation, there are two different methods for obtaining this data, both of which are heavily influenced by jurisdictional privacy regulations in place:

- **Silent capture** – this process records the customer-side audio from many calls over a period. These recordings are then annotated with an anonymised customer identifier (the calls from the same customer receive the same identifier). This audio is likely to contain imposters, so it may require a manual review, but it is the most representative of the caller base. It is likely that some customers will have made repeat calls during this period, which can provide higher confidence in the FR performance results, if only for that short period of time.
  In this case, the customer's audio is used for the purpose of obtaining data only. Any voiceprint created is not associated with the customer and will subsequently be destroyed, but this process may still not be compliant with the privacy legislation in some jurisdictions.

- **Registered customers** – this process is dependent on the customer having enrolled and subsequently called back several times. After the customer has registered, it may take some time before they have made enough repeat calls to give you high confidence in the FR performance results.

When you're using registered customers to tune and calibrate the voice-biometrics system, design the Crawl, Walk, Run implementation approach to capture sufficient audio from each phase and allow enough time to process and implement the improved algorithms before moving on to the next phase.

Using out-of-the-box settings without calibration during the Crawl phase means that the performance characteristics are not fully understood and the risk of FA is unknown, so it is unwise to involve real customers at this point without some safeguards. I often refer to this phase as 'friends and family', as employees and potentially their close contacts can be invited to call a dedicated number on which the new process has been implemented. In some cases, it may even be appropriate to retain the existing security process as a safety measure.

These 'customers' can be registered. After registration, they can be encouraged to call several times with different tasks, and even from different devices and locations to increase the diversity of the sample. This should provide you with a big enough sample on which to tune and calibrate your technology.

Unfortunately, many workforces (particularly employees of the call centre itself) are not representative of the organisation's customer base in terms of age, gender and regional accents. While the Crawl phase does provide a baseline view, the Walk phase can supply a more representative sample. Once you've established the scope of your technology and gained confidence in the business processes, I recommend expanding your tests to a representative group of customers. The challenge here is that once a customer is registered, they will expect to receive the new experience.

The best solution is to select a small line of business where all the calls are handled by the same agent group. Alternatively, train between 5 and 10% of a larger group of agents in the new registration and authentication process, and the remainder of agents just in the authentication process.

The tuning and calibration results from the Walk phase will give you sufficient confidence to establish the initial operating threshold and expand registration to more customers. As your data was obtained over a relatively short period of time, there is a risk that the rate of FRs could increase as customers' voices change over time, so monitor the mismatch rate for this. You may be able to increase overall performance with additional tuning once you have had a significant increase in data.

Tuning and calibration for network authentication

Network-data authentication and fraud detection have a limited privacy impact on customers, so tuning and calibration can use data from all calls received. Initial calibration can therefore be completed with only a few days' or weeks' worth of data.

Unlike voice biometrics, other callers' data cannot be used to simulate imposters. It is important to identify, using other methods, all suspicious or fraudulent calls so that their data can be used to further train the algorithms. As with voice biometrics, most vendors' models will perform well out of the box, but there are always idiosyncrasies and variations in individual organisations' customers and calls that benefit from both positive (feeding back on calls that are known to be the correct caller/device) and negative (feeding back on known fraudulent calls) reinforcement.

Establishing postures and thresholds

The calibration process generates an understanding of the relative FA and FR rates for each score, but to implement the authentication method, you need to decide on what the appropriate threshold score should be.

For simplicity of stakeholder understanding and getting agreement from them, I recommend you select a single authentication threshold that balances your organisation's appetite for risk with efficiency and usability. While it is possible to specify different handling for different scores, such as those just below the threshold or those significantly above it, this creates more complexity for relatively little marginal gain. This doesn't mean that you shouldn't have a separate threshold for calls highly likely to be fraudulent which may be subject to different treatment.

It's essential for those closest to the new application, such as those who will be managing it day to day in your own teams, to understand the results of a typical calibration exercise, but they can be hard for more remote stakeholders to grasp. When discussing the threshold with these stakeholders, avoid using specific numbers until you have results based on your own data. Instead, discuss the threshold in terms of posture. This allows everyone to understand that there is a trade-off and enables more principles-based decision making that can later be tested with real numbers.

In practice, there are only three operating postures:

- **Security focused** – in this posture, using all the benefits of modern authentication to improve security, you prioritise minimising the number of FAs within the constraint of a maximum acceptable number of FRs (usually similar to the level experienced with traditional authentication methods). This threshold is often the point on the curve where any further reduction in the FA rate will have a disproportionate impact on the FR rate.

- **Balanced** – in this posture, you attempt to get the best of both worlds by minimising both FA and FR rates. Within the constraints of the curve, this point is usually found around the apex (as shown in Figure 14.4).

- **Experience focused** – in this posture, you prioritise minimising the number of FRs within the constraint of maximum acceptable number of FAs (usually similar to the level experienced with traditional authentication methods). This threshold is often the point on the curve where any further reduction in the FR rate will have a disproportionate impact on the FA rate.

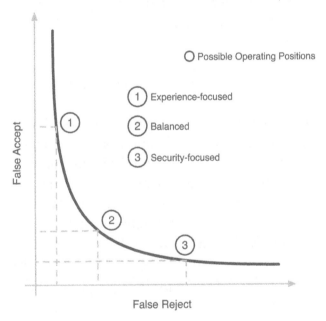

Figure 14.4: Operating postures

In practice, these postures describe the ends and middle of a range, but discussing the threshold in these terms helps all stakeholders agree the rough positioning in advance of deciding on real numbers. I find that organisations will naturally gravitate towards one of these postures based on the nature of their products and services as well as their competitive positioning. Most financial services organisations, for example, will favour a security-focused position, while public-sector organisations may be more experience focused.

Consider how your organisation's posture might change over time. It is, for example, perfectly appropriate to adopt a more security-focused posture initially, with an expectation of moving towards a balanced posture after you have gained confidence and data to validate the processes.

When the results of tuning and calibration are available, the conversation can switch from hypothetical to practical, but the results of these exercises and the specific trade-offs are not easy for everyone to understand. Agree the posture at a strategic level, but delegate the specific threshold decision to those most directly responsible for the outcomes.

To support delegation, you may find it useful to define more objective metrics, such as the reported number of FAs or associated fraud incidents, which are easy for everyone to understand. Those closest to the front-line can then continue to make changes and adjust thresholds within this constraint without needing further stakeholder discussion.

Estimating FA volumes

For many organisations, the key performance metric for a new authentication method will be the number of FAs, so the process of determining a threshold needs to estimate this to ensure it is at a level everyone is comfortable with. The results of the calibration will provide you with the expected rate of FAs at different thresholds. Alongside an estimate of the number of fraudulent calls and attacks, you can then identify the likely number of fraudster FAs, but remember that this is only an estimate, based on the quality of the calibration sample.

FAs can come from more than just fraudsters attempting to gain access; genuine customers can ask friends and relatives to attempt to do the same. In my experience, genuine customers often try to test the service soon after their initial registration. Of these, the vast majority conduct some form of positive test to make sure it works for them and only a small minority attempt their own imposter tests.

Unfortunately, because the genuine customer often does these tests with relatives (who may have some genetic similarities) or friends (who may have some behavioural similarities, such as accent) and using the same device that they used to register, their 'imposter' is, on average, more likely to be successful than another customer selected at random (as represented in the calibration results). As a realistic estimate, I assume that the customer's test imposters may be up to five times more likely to achieve an FA. Fortunately, it is likely that the genuine customer will then contact you to complain or report the incident, providing more valuable feedback.

You can use my online calculator at www.symnexconsulting.com/unlock-book to estimate the number of FAs for your organisation.

Summary

To deliver on the promise of modern security, you must ensure that the system operates as expected, you get the right balance of speed and quality during implementation, and frontline colleagues are as well prepared as possible to introduce the new service to customers. In this chapter, we have covered a framework for planning implementation that offers the optimal balance of these competing demands and enables effective decision making.

The main points we've looked at are:

- The key areas of focus during implementation are the core customer journeys, authentication performance and your organisation's requirement for supporting processes.

- Use the Crawl, Walk, Run approach to test and understand the elements of implementation in a controlled environment before gradually introducing the new system to customers.

- Make sure your frontline agents are trained in your new processes and have the chance to practise using them. There will be opportunities for them to improve on the job, but it's easier to give them a strong start.

- The key frontline-agent training requirements for voice biometrics are understanding of the process, awareness of the positioning of the offer appropriate for different customers and objection handling.

- Calibration (understanding performance) and tuning (improving performance) will enable you to identify the correct balance between security and convenience for your organisation. Obtain the data necessary for tuning and calibration in the Crawl and Walk phases.

- You should establish your preferred postures to facilitate threshold decision making, weighing up the degree to which they need to be security focused, balanced or experience focused.

15

Optimisation

Implementation is just the start of the process. As you learn from your experience with modern security, there will be opportunities to optimise the performance of both your business processes and the underlying technology. You also need to ensure that you support your customers throughout their lifecycle and be prepared for the inevitable situation where security breaches occur.

In this chapter, I will provide you with a methodology to sustain and increase the value of the processes you introduce.

Measuring and improving process performance

As you progress through each phase of implementation, you need to measure and understand how the end-to-end process is performing. It should be possible to use existing data to baseline your expected performance before launch, and then validate this during the Crawl and Walk phases of implementation.

The key metrics to consider are:

- **Legacy identification and authentication rate** – you should have a good understanding of these from your initial assessment, but the reality may still vary from your expectations. This is particularly the case if some time has passed since the assessment or if certain authentication methods are ineligible for enrolment.

- **Registration rate** – at the highest level, this is the proportion of unregistered authenticated callers who are registered on a call. For network authentication, this is simply the number of new numbers obtained, but the process for voice biometrics is significantly more involved (see next section).

Figure 15.1: *Registration and authentication value chain*

- **Registered customer identification rate** – this is the rate at which registered customers return and are identified, which is dependent on caller frequency. This can be especially hard to forecast as most organisations only measure this number over a year. In my experience, initial rates and increases are likely to overestimate the medium-term trend as the number of newly registered customers testing the service outweighs the number of established customers returning for legitimate reasons.

- **Registered customer authentication rate (match rate)** – the rate at which these returning customers are authenticated can be inferred from the results of the calibration process, but this does exclude TRs. During the early phases of implementation, it is helpful to sample mismatch results and categorise them as either FRs or TRs to understand the genuine level of the registered customer authentication rate.

CASE STUDY: VALUE OF METRICS

Time and again, the importance of robust value-chain measurement has been proved to me during service launches.

When I worked for an international bank, the data told us that despite customers being enrolled, they were not being authenticated when they called back. We ultimately traced this to a misconfigured router in a remote office that resulted in calls bypassing the audio-capture process.

An investment manager was able to quantify the impact of known system defects outside the scope of the security process that had been de-prioritised for fixing because they were thought to be minor. As they could now express the downstream impact in terms of enrolled customers and missed authentication opportunities, the issues were prioritised and quickly fixed.

Working with another financial services firm, I soon identified that a decision made during the design process, expected to have a minor effect, was having a significant impact on registration volumes. Again, because it was clear what the customer impact was, the organisation was able to reverse the policy decision quickly and ensure more customers had access to the service.

With a retail bank, I took this process further and added measurement steps for each of its risk countermeasures. I then used this data to express the cost of these controls on customers versus the risks they were mitigating, ultimately resulting in these controls being removed or significantly moderated.

Measuring voice-biometrics registration

Adding the registration process steps into the value chain for voice biometrics gives a fuller perspective of how each individual step performs.

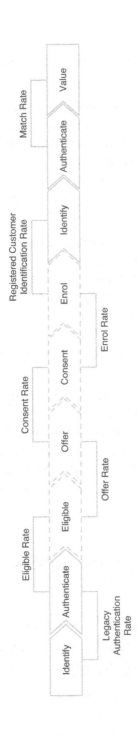

Figure 15.2: Voice-biometrics value-chain metrics

There are two key metrics that cannot be established during the design phase, so make measuring these your focus during the Walk phase. Measure both these metrics in aggregate and at an agent, team and business unit level as rates are likely to vary, sometimes significantly, across the agent population.

The two key metrics are:

- **Eligible to offer (offer rate)** – this is the rate at which eligible customers are presented with an offer to enrol by an agent. It's almost entirely an agent's responsibility. Their willingness to make the offer will be influenced by their training, incentives, user-interface choices and your process design decisions, such as the point on the call to make the offer.

  You will be able to increase this rate over time with appropriate coaching and incentives, but if the initial rates are lower than your expectations, review agent training, messaging and incentives to identify opportunities to improve. I have found that this rate is heavily influenced by agents' belief in the value of the service, so it helps to provide them with an opportunity to try it out and hear feedback on the value from real customers.

- **Offer to consent (consent rate)** – this is the rate at which customers accept the offer and provide their consent, and it is heavily influenced by the level of agent skill in positioning and selling the benefits of the new service. There are many reasons why customers may not give their consent, but the initial rates achieved by the upper quartile of agents provide a good estimate of achievable rates in the medium term, with suitable coaching and incentives.

If these rates are lower than your expectations, it will be worth a more detailed analysis of the most frequent reasons for customers withholding consent. This is best done by asking them directly using surveys or outbound calls by members of your project team.

These two metrics usually provide the greatest opportunity to improve process performance during implementation, but ensure that you understand how the other process steps are performing. They too need to be consistent with your expectations, bearing in mind that improving their performance may require more fundamental changes to the design.

These process steps are:

- **Eligibility rate** – this is the rate at which customers who have been identified and authenticated are eligible to be offered enrolment. Again, you should be able to estimate this in advance, but if you haven't done so, the initial implementation phases will be your opportunity. If the rate is lower than expected, review the most frequently occurring reasons why customers are not eligible to ensure they are appropriate and not a result of poor data or misunderstanding.

- **Consent to enrolment (enrol rate)** – this is the rate at which customers who provide consent are successfully enrolled, which is influenced by the amount of time they speak on a call and configuration decisions about the minimum amount of audio needed to enrol them. There may be technical reasons why this rate could be lower than expected, so review it with your technology supplier if relevant.

Managing agent performance

Habits and patterns are hard to break, but not impossible. In my experience of working with thousands of agents across two continents and dozens of sites, it takes a lot of work to significantly improve individual agent performance once they have settled into a pattern, so it pays to invest in giving agents the best start possible. While a single training intervention can provide agents with the knowledge required, developing skill invariably requires feedback and coaching.

I recommend that team leaders or coaches monitor, remotely or in person, agents' first offer and consent attempts with real customers. Immediately after the call, they can ask the agent to assess their own performance and provide advice for improvement. This process should continue for a handful of calls until the agent is confident and performing at the level expected.

In my experience, this initial focused effort has proven time and again to sustain the highest levels of agent registration performance. Several years later, a distinct difference in performance remains between two parts of one organisation that took different approaches to training during implementation.

Following initial implementation of the new security process, there will inevitably be variations in performance across the frontline-agent population. This is where you use offer, consent and enrolment metrics on an individual agent basis to identify and diagnose issues. Team leaders and coaches can use this data not only to focus their efforts on those agents requiring support, but also to identify pockets of best practice that they can share with others.

Supporting processes

In addition to the core registration and authentication processes, you will need supporting business processes for a range of exceptions. In many cases, these processes will arise in response to customer requests, but there is an opportunity to initiate some of them proactively.

A small proportion of customers will experience difficulties using the service because of a poor quality or incorrect enrolment (although they won't know that). Having failed to authenticate several times, these customers are likely to ask agents to disable the service, but this is often an opportunity to repair or correct the defect. Wherever possible, the agent should placate these customers and ask for permission to investigate the problems and repair any faults before deregistration.

You will need a subject-matter expert with access to the backend systems to investigate and understand the cause of the issue and fix it where possible. They often need to review the original registration to ensure that it is the correct customer experiencing the difficulties and there are no obvious issues with it. If there are, for voice biometrics, they may be able to use audio from other calls to replace it and re-enrol the customer without further intervention, but if the reason is unclear or there is a risk that the real customer did not give consent, agents need to ask the customer to complete registration again.

As most customer issues are a result of repeated authentication failures and customer tolerance of these will vary, there is an opportunity to use reporting to identify issues before most customers complain. In many cases, it will be easier and more efficient to resolve issues in bulk rather than individually, and the pay-off will be an increase in overall authentication rates.

There will, of course, be situations where customers don't want to continue using the service even if they don't experience any issues. In most cases, privacy legislation requires that you provide a mechanism for customers to opt out and have their voiceprint deleted or number disabled for authentication. This process is best carried out by a subject-matter expert as there is a small risk that it could be exploited by fraudsters.

Plan for every eventuality

Given the probabilistic nature of modern authentication, it is inevitable that at some point, you will experience an FA. For organisations handling millions of calls a year, it is a mathematical certainty.

In my experience, it is often only when this happens that the relative understanding of all the stakeholders becomes clear. You might have known all along this was almost certain to happen, but some stakeholders may, despite your best efforts, have a false mental model of probabilistic authentication and incorrectly assume it means FAs will never happen. Consequently, there is a huge risk that an organisation will overreact to FAs, which is why it is essential to have a clear and agreed plan for this eventuality. Many call centres already have well-established processes for managing incidents which, if possible, I would advise you to follow.

As we have discussed previously, FAs are likely to stem from one of two situations: a real fraud or a genuine customer colluding with a friend or relative to test your system. Even in organisations with a high rate of fraudster attack, the more likely occurrences are from genuine customers. As a result, the first report of an FA will probably come from a customer to an agent, so a mechanism must exist for the agent to report this for investigation.

To support the investigation, it's critical that the agent captures as much information as possible about what happened and when, including what the customer wants your organisation to do about it. As agents are only human, it's likely they will tell colleagues and supervisors about the incident, so ensure you are upfront about the risk posed by FAs. Then an instance of FA won't undermine agent advocacy, which is so important to successful registration.

As you don't want your stakeholders to hear about FAs as a rumour before you've updated them, the next step after identification of an FA is to notify all interested parties that an incident has occurred, you are investigating and when you expect to update them next. The investigation obviously needs to be prioritised and will require you or a subject-matter expert to listen to any available call recordings to determine whether this is an FA and whether it creates any cause for concern that the process is not working as expected.

In most cases, the incident can be safely closed as an FA within the appetite agreed during the threshold-setting process and you can update stakeholders accordingly. Other issues may require further investigation with your technology provider.

An FA that actually involves an imposter is most likely to be identified during a fraud investigation associated with an authentication. In this case, you or a subject-matter expert should review the records and any recordings associated with the customer to identify whether the incident is a true FA or, more likely, an imposter having been enrolled and subsequently authenticated because of vulnerabilities in the authentication method used during registration of either voiceprint or phone number. In the case of a true FA, evaluate it as to whether it is within the appetite for risk you agreed with stakeholders during threshold setting or whether it is cause for greater concern, which may require changes to thresholds and/or investigation with your technology provider.

CASE STUDY: RITE OF PASSAGE

While organisations may go several months or even years before experiencing one of these issues, I consider the successful handling of the first such incident to be a rite of passage to a true modern security process. Here are a few examples from my experience:

- Following a case where an employee asked their twin to break into their account, a European bank had a far better understanding of the risks from customer testing.

- When a customer of a North American investment manager passed their phone across their garden fence to a friend and asked him to be an imposter, the organisation gained a far greater understanding of how regional accents affected the performance of their system.

- When an employee of a third party was able to authenticate as a customer, a UK bank was able to identify issues with its registration process.

Sometimes the organisation had a plan and executed it well, but on many occasions, they responded reactively. Either way, though, the process and organisation became stronger as a result of the experience.

Managing vulnerabilities

Modern security methods are probabilistic and allow organisations to fine-tune their appetite for risk based on the probability of incorrectly accepting an imposter. That said, you need to ensure you understand and appropriately mitigate the range of vulnerabilities that may confound this relationship. Some vulnerabilities may allow fraudsters to attack the very features of a system that provide its strength, but generally it is far easier to bypass them and exploit known weaknesses in traditional and transitional methods.

The low FA rates of a voice-biometrics system discourage fraudsters from attacking the system directly and encourage them to bypass it entirely. The fact that a proportion of genuine customers will be incorrectly rejected (FRs) can be exploited by fraudsters who are correctly rejected (TRs) as the distinction cannot be determined on the call. Ensure that any fallback process restricts the range of services available to these callers to those with an appropriate level of risk or puts in place additional measures (including detective measures) for the minority of callers in this situation who require access to higher-risk services.

All biometrics systems are vulnerable to replay or presentation attacks, in which a fraudster obtains a sample from the genuine customer and presents this to the authentication process. For voice biometrics, this is done through recordings. Fortunately, where the authentication takes place alongside an agent conversation and that conversation continues beyond the point of authentication, it is easy for the agent to identify recordings. The fraudster is highly unlikely to be able to capture sufficient speech from the genuine customer and replay it in a natural enough way to dupe the agent, unless there is collusion with the genuine customer.

Where authentication is unattended, such as in an automated system, review the techniques available from your technology vendor to identify recordings and other suspicious behaviour before providing access to higher-risk services. There is also a risk that recordings could be used in an automated system for authentication before the fraudster speaks to an agent, so always continue or repeat authentication on the agent part of the call.

A further development of this risk is the emergence of synthetic voices powered by machine learning that use samples of a real person's voice to create a model. This can then be used to say anything. These synthetic voices often require a large amount of specific audio from the targeted speaker, making them only viable as a form of attack on high-profile customers who have a significant amount of audio recordings in the public domain. As today's synthetic voices are optimised to sound like humans (eg voice assistants like Alexa) rather than a biometric comparison, they can usually be easily identified by tell-tale artefacts the process leaves behind.

It is good practice, therefore, to carry out a regular thorough vulnerability assessment of both individual methods and the overall system to identify and mitigate the highest-risk issues. As technology continues to evolve, the sophistication of both attackers and mitigation methods will increase, so you must have a means to stay abreast of these developments.

Summary

As you learn from your experience with modern security, there will be opportunities to optimise the performance of both your business processes and the underlying technology, ensuring that you support your customers and are prepared for the inevitable situation where security breaches occur. We have looked in this chapter at the methodology to sustain and increase the value of the security processes you introduce.

The key points we've covered are:

- Continuous measurement and analysis of performance will highlight opportunities for improvement.

- Monitoring the key metrics aligned with the value chain will help you understand your performance. The key metrics are legacy identification and authentication rate, registration rate, registered customer identification rate and registered customer authentication rate.

- There are two key measures for voice-biometrics registration that cannot be established during the design phase, so make improving these your focus during the Walk and Run phases. These key measures are eligible to offer (offer rate) and offer to consent (consent rate).

- Team leaders or coaches need to monitor agents' first offer and consent attempts with real customers. They can then ask the agent to assess their own performance and provide advice for improvement.

- In addition to the core registration and authentication processes, you will need supporting business processes for a range of exceptions.

- No security process can be guaranteed to prevent all attacks, so you need to be prepared for predictable incidents. You also need to make all stakeholders aware that FAs within certain parameters will still occur.

- Understand the inherent vulnerabilities and remain vigilant to emerging ones with appropriate plans in place to mitigate them.

Conclusion

I will never forget late one Wednesday night. I was leaving a Glasgow call centre, about to head out into the wet and windy streets after everything had calmed down following a weekend implementation of a modern security process, when a young lady I had never met before stopped me in the lift and thanked me for changing her life.

While 'changing her life' may have been a bit of an exaggeration, she was genuinely relieved that I had removed the thing that made her feel least like coming to work every day. She hated that she couldn't help her customers until after she'd put them through a knowledge-based authentication dance where both parties knew there was no real security provided. Over the next few months, I saw first-hand with this organisation that when you get security out of the way and release the potential of your people to serve your customers, magic happens.

The fundamental challenges detailed in Part One are the same for all, but how they manifest to affect the usability, efficiency and security performance of your process is not. No organisation is the same as another. Each will have individual complexities and idiosyncrasies that void any prescriptive recommendation. In Part Two I provided an approach, framework and tools to guide and support you to determine the right answer for your organisation. If you have any doubt about where to start, it's with visualising your current performance. Time and again, the relatively little effort required to complete this step proves its worth by building collective understanding and momentum towards improvement.

As you start to implement modern security, you will need to balance the competing needs of customers, different stakeholders and the reality of the technology. In Part Three I provided you with my hard-won best practice, but of course these too will need to be tailored for your unique context. The effort will be worth it. Your customers and your agents will thank you and you will start to feel the value of unlocking your call centre's full potential.

Over the next few years, I expect to see the technologies we've discussed in this book mature, lowering the cost of entry to the point where there is no rational reason not to adopt them. They will increasingly appear as features or add-ons to call-centre platforms, reducing the complexity of integration and cost further. I am excited about the potential for these technologies, including behavioural analytics, to work more seamlessly together not just in a single call, but across all customer touchpoints. Then security processes can truly disappear into the background and only come to the fore on the few occasions they are really needed, allowing agents to focus on the most important part of their job: your customers. Beyond the call centre, these and other technologies will be applied in similar ways to remove the friction from authentication processes of all sorts while delivering more secure customer interactions.

My personal mission is to improve the call centre security experience for every customer. By distilling what I have learned in this book, it's my genuine hope that thousands more organisations than I could hope to impact through my consulting engagements will be able to upgrade their security. My website – www. symnexconsulting.com/unlock-book – is packed with additional resources to help you, including diagnostic assessments, templates, in-depth articles, educational videos and supplier directories. Together, they provide everything you need to start unlocking the potential of your call centres without any further help from me. And I'd love to hear how you get on.

You may still need help getting started or dealing with particularly complex or urgent challenges. Through my consulting engagements, I help organisations get better results quicker and with less effort than they could achieve on their own. If this sounds like it could help you, then I am available for no-obligation exploration calls through www.symnexconsulting.com.

Appendix: Acronyms

You can find a full glossary on my website: www.symnexconsulting.com/glossary.

ANI – automatic number identification

B2B – business-to-business

CLI – caller line identification

CRM – customer relationship management

FA – false accept

FR – false reject

IVR – interactive voice response

NLU – natural language understanding

OTP – one-time passcode

PIN – personal identification number

ROI – return on investment

SIM – subscriber identity module

SMS – short message service

TR – true reject

TUIT – true user imposter test

Acknowledgements

There are a number of people I would like to take this opportunity to thank. Firstly, my managers at two pivotal moments in my career: Shane Greene, Marc Finch, Jamie Paterson and Anne Grim, who trusted me with the space and resources to pursue what others would have dismissed, and the soldiers of Training Team Bravo and Iain Hanlon, who had my back while giving me the honest and sometimes direct feedback I needed to stay on the right path. I would have learned none of what I've shared in this book without them.

All of SymNex Consulting's clients and partners have shaped my thinking and pushed me to improve in different ways, but Dan Miller, Andrea Ayres, Carsten Miller, Fred Bishop and Brett Beranek deserve particular recognition for their vision, insight and camaraderie.

Thanks go to Hamish Stewart of Flare Design, Dan Miller of Opus Research (who also wrote the foreword) and Nick Powell of Stronger Self for their feedback and encouragement after reading early versions of this book. Also to the team at Rethink Press, particularly Lucy McCarraher and Joe Gregory for their excellent Bookbuilder book and programme which provided the structure and discipline to write this book, and Verity Ridgman for keeping me accountable and providing literally thousands of suggestions for improvement.

My wife, Charlie, has been by my side for this whole journey and been unequivocal in her support through the highs and lows. She has been constantly serene, giving me permission and support to do my own thing even when our family's financial security was at stake. Finally, thank you to my son Thomas, who never doubted I would finish this book, thereby ensuring that I had to.

Thank you all!

The Author

Matt Smallman has always been driven to solve problems that others believed were unsolvable through the application of advanced technology and the understanding of human behaviour. He started his career as a British Army officer, joining the Corps of Royal Engineers. After an operational tour in Afghanistan, he chose to specialise in counter-terrorist search operations, ultimately redesigning and leading delivery of pre-deployment training for thousands of soldiers from the UK and other NATO nations heading to Iraq and Afghanistan.

After starting a second career in financial services, he focused on customer-experience strategy and call-centre technology, leading various teams at two of the UK's largest banks. It was in these roles that he saw first-hand the impact of poor security processes on every dimension of performance, which led him to design and deliver the first modern security experiences for customers of the UK's largest wealth manager.

Five years later, frustrated that so few organisations had followed the path he'd illuminated, he founded SymNex Consulting to help organisations improve the usability, efficiency and security of their customer-service operations by transforming their processes. At SymNex, he has led the design and implementation of modern security processes for several of the world's most customer-centric brands covering tens of millions of customers in North America and Europe.

A graduate of Warwick Business School, Matt is a keen but still novice endurance runner hoping to get more competitive as he ages. He lives in Winchester, Hampshire with his wife Charlie and son Thomas.

You can get in touch with Matt and find out more about his work via:

⊕ www.symnexconsulting.com

in www.linkedin.com/in/mattsmallman